A Christmas Gift to
my husband.
John R. Offinger

Dec 25" 1881.

Bloomington
Ill.

THE

HOPES OF THE HUMAN RACE,

HEREAFTER AND HERE.

THE

HOPES OF THE HUMAN RACE,

HEREAFTER AND HERE.

BY

FRANCES POWER COBBE.

NEW YORK:
JAMES MILLER, PUBLISHER,
779 BROADWAY.

CONTENTS.

PAGE

PREFACE (HAVING SPECIAL REFERENCE TO MR. MILL'S ESSAY ON RELIGION) 9

THE LIFE AFTER DEATH. PART I. 73

THE LIFE AFTER DEATH. PART II. . . . 127

DOOMED TO BE SAVED. AN ADDRESS . . . 183

THE EVOLUTION OF THE SOCIAL SENTIMENT . 209

PREFACE.

PREFACE.

The principal essay in this book addresses itself to a small class of readers. For those who believe that a life after death has been guaranteed to mankind by a supernatural revelation, it is superfluous; and for those who believe that the experiences of the bodily senses, and the inductions thence derived, mark the limits of human knowledge, it is useless. There yet remain some minds to whom I hope the speculations and observations which it contains may not be uninteresting or unserviceable; who, having lost faith in the apocalyptic side of Christianity, find no basis therein for their immortal hopes, but who are yet able to trust the spiritual instincts of their own and other men's hearts, provided they can recognize the direction in which they harmoniously point. I indulge no dream of discovering new ground for faith in immortality, still less of proving that we are immortal by logical demonstration. But something will be gained, if I succeed in warning off a few inquirers from false paths which lead only to disappointment, and point out to them, if not the true argument, yet the true *method* of argument, whereby such satisfaction as lies within our reach may be obtained. Perhaps I may have the greater advantage in speaking of the belief in a future life, because for many years of my own earlier life, while slowly regaining faith in God after the collapse of supernaturalism, I failed to discover any sufficient reason for such trust, and, in the desire to be loyal to truth, deliberately thrust it away even under the pressure of a great sorrow. It is possible, therefore, that I may understand better than most believers in the doctrine why many honest, and not irreligious, minds are at this moment mournfully shutting out that gleam of a brighter world which should cheer and glorify the present; and perhaps I may also have learned from experience how some of their difficulties may be met.

It is needless to discuss the importance of the belief of mankind in a life beyond the grave. Whether, with a recent distinguished writer, we look on the threatened loss of it as the most perilous of our "rocks ahead," on which the whole order of society may make shipwreck; or whether (as I am more disposed to think) the danger lies in the gradual *carnalization* of our nature which would follow the extinction of those ennobling hopes which have lifted men above mere animalism, and given to duty and to love an infinite extension, — in either case, it is hard to speak too gravely of the imperilment of that which has been, since the beginning of history, perhaps the most precious of the mental heirlooms of our race. To conjure up a picture of the desolation which such a loss must bring to the hearts of the bereaved, and the dreary hopelessness of the dying and the aged, would be to give ourselves superfluous pain. Nor must it be forgotten that it does not ask a great deal, if not to *kill* such a faith (which is perhaps impossible), yet to maim and paralyze it, so that it shall become practically powerless to comfort or to elevate. The great majority of mankind rather *catch* belief and disbelief from those around them than originate them on their own account; and the disbelief of even a few of their neighbors is often sufficient to take away all confidence in the affirmative verdict even of the wisest and best. Dr. Johnson said he was "injured by knowing there was one man who did not believe in Christianity:" the knowledge was just so far a deduction from the universality of consent in which even that intellectual giant found repose. It would probably need only that five per cent of the population should publish their conviction that there is no future state, to make the greater part of the remainder so far lose reliance upon it as to become quite insensible to its moral influences.

But while thoughtful persons are generally agreed on the great importance of the doctrine in question, it has, perhaps, scarcely been noticed how it is inevitably destined to form the turning-point of the future religious history of our race. The dogma of a future life differs from other articles of faith notably in being indissoluble in the alembic of interpretation wherein so many of our more solid beliefs have of recent years been rarefied into thin air. "To be, or not to be," is very literally the question of questions, to which must needs be given a categorical response. Either we ourselves, in innermost identity, shall exist after the mortal hour, or we shall not so exist: there is no third contingency. With respect to our faith in God, there are immeasurable shades between the definite and fervent conviction of the existence of a true Father in heaven, and the admission that there lies behind Nature some "unknown and unknowable" Mind, Will, or perchance blind and unintelligent Force, which we choose to call by the same sacred name. Owing to the voluntary and involuntary obscurities of human language, and the dimness of human thought, there will always exist a misty territory between the confines of theism and atheism; and it may be only too easy to slip down imperceptibly, range after range, from one to the other, only discovering at last how far we have descended, when the sunlight which shone on the mountain-tops has faded away utterly among the dark shadows of the abyss. But there is scarcely any such danger of thus playing fast and loose with our beliefs as regards immortality. It is true, that among those alchemists of creeds of whom I have already spoken, many of whom can find the pure gold of moral truth in every base and heavy superstition, while others concoct an elixir of life out of the hellebore and the nightshade of denial and despair, there have not failed to be some who have taught that man, if mortal in the concrete, and doomed individually to perish in the dust, may yet call himself an immortal being; immortal, that is, in his abstract humanity, in the *grand-être* of which he forms a part, and which will survive the falling-off of such a mere fraction of it as himself; or (if this consolation be not amply sufficient) that he will yet live in his posterity, in his works of beneficence, in the books wherewith he may have instructed mankind. But even to very sanguine souls it must (I should suppose) be nearly hopeless thus to attempt to give the change to our personal hopes and desires concerning a life after death, by reminding us of hopes for other people, which, far from being a novel equivalent for our own, have always hitherto been taken as concurrent therewith and additional thereto; and which actually bring with them, when the doctrine of individual immortality is denied, only the mournful question of how far it may remain an object of hope at all that a race should prolong its existence when every soul which composes it is destined to perish incomplete, unfinished, a failure, like the ill-turned vase which the potter casts aside on the heap to be broken up as worthless. There can be truly, then, only the response of Ay or No to the question, "When a man dieth, shall he live again?" And on the decision, whether most men say "Ay," or say "No," will depend, in yet undreamed-of measure, the moral condition of coming generations.

In the following essay I have stated to the best of my ability the grounds on which I think an affirmative answer to the great enigma may be given by all those who believe in a *righteous* as well as an *intelligent* Ruler of the world. I have no desire to blink the fact that it is on the moral attributes of God that the whole question appears to me to hinge; and that, without the help of religion (of a real religion, which takes for its corner-stone that God is good and just, not a philosophy which merely admits the hypothesis of an intelligent force behind Nature), the reasons for denial seem to me to preponderate altogether over those in favor of affirmation.

But here is the great, the tremendous difficulty. How is that belief in the righteousness and benevolence of God to be established so as that we may build thereon securely our hopes of a life to come? Nay, how is it, in these days of earthquake, to be kept firm enough for the purpose — higher even than of affording us immortal hope — of giving us *now* a Father in heaven to adore, and in allegiance to whose holy will we may be content to live and die? It is impossible to hide from ourselves, that the obstacles in the way of a clear faith in the absolute goodness of God have grievously multiplied upon us in our generation. Perhaps genuine fidelity should call on us to rejoice that they have also, at last, found a most lucid and coherent expression in the mournful legacy left us by the great philosopher lately departed, wherein the yet formless questionings, the "ghastliest doubts," of thousands of souls have taken shape, and will stand revealed to themselves like the Afrit out of the smoke. Of this book I must speak presently. Let it be remarked, in passing, that Mr. Mill has, not unnaturally, read all the religious history of mankind in the peculiar light of his own exceptional mental experience, and has taken it for granted that men have, in all ages, constructed a God by the method of the inductive philosophy. I venture to think that an entirely opposite *rationale* of religious development is the true one, and that, by recognizing it, we may exactly perceive how it happens that we have arrived at our present pass.

Mankind, I believe, from the hour when humanity arose out of its purely animal origin, has felt some vague stirrings of aspiration and awe; some infant-like liftings-up of the hands for help and pity to something greater, stronger, wiser, than itself; some dim consciousness (enough, at least, to guide its funeral-rites) that it is not all of a man which perishes in the grave. Long ages and millenniums, doubtless, passed away, during which these vague sentiments fastened on some fetich, or on the orbs of heaven, at first without ascribing any definite individuality or personality to the object, and then, again, without attributing to it any moral character. In the " ages before morality," the gods were necessarily unmoral; for man could no more invent morality to give his god than he could invent for him a bodily sense which he did not himself possess. But with the dawnings of the ethical sentiment in man came simultaneously the conviction, nay, rather, the consciousness, that the Unseen Power was also just (so far as the man yet apprehended justice). Thenceforward the moral ideal of God continued to rise, century after century, in exact proportion to the moral development of mankind; and the "Lord" was a pillar of cloud and fire, moving before the moving nations, guiding them towards the Holy Land. It mattered little that it was, for the masses, in the shape of the intuitions of dead prophets and apostles, which were called divine inspirations (and *were* so in truth, albeit mixed with endless fables), that Jews and Zoroastrians, Christians and Moslems, accepted this inward idea of God, and only a few of the "strongest souls" received (as the old Chaldæan oracle has it) "light through themselves." Practically, mankind at large held, more or less imperfectly, the notion of Deity reflected from the highest consciousness yet developed at each stage; and, poor as it often was, it was the brightest which could filter through the dim windows of their souls. The work of correcting this ideal by reference to the phenomena of Nature, instead of being the normal process, hardly seems to have occurred to any one save Lucretius. When these phenomena were beneficent and beautiful, men sung psalms, and proclaimed that the heavens declared the glory of God, and the earth was full of his goodness. When plague and earthquake, flood and famine, ravaged the world, they attributed the evil to the wrath of the higher powers, brought down by the offences of mankind, of which there never was an insufficient store to serve for such explanation. It is even surprising, in our day, to note how very remote it was from the spirit of old philosophers or theologians to put aside *à priori* doctrines about the gods, and learn from Nature herself concerning Nature's Authorship. Even down to the days of Paley and the Bridgewater Treatises, it is clear that, when they applied to Nature at all, it was as a French judge sometimes interrogates a prisoner, to compel her to corroborate their foregone conclusions respecting a series of "attributes," either apprehended by the religious sentiment, or logically deduced by the *à priori* arguments of the schoolmen. There were, doubtless, abundant reasons for this state of things. The poets, the artists, the sages of old, cared comparatively little about Nature, and centred all their interest in man. As it has been wittily said, "Nature was only discovered in our generation." It followed obviously, then, that the theologians of former times should concern themselves almost exclusively with the human aspects of religion and the notions of dead thinkers, and that only now and then some great teacher arose to rebuke the servile repetition of what was "said by them of old time," and to point to the lilies of the field and the birds of the air as evidence of the Father's love.

But our age witnesses a new tendency of thought altogether, — the genuine application of the inductive philosophy to theology. With the vast and sudden influx of knowledge concerning the outer world, has come a greatly enhanced sense of the importance of the inferences to be drawn therefrom regarding the character of its Author, and the purpose of his work. Some of us are now at the stage of seeking in Nature the corroboration of our intuitive faith; others, of painfully balancing the two revelations; and others, yet again, have gone so far as to look exclusively to astronomy and geology, and chemistry and physiology, to afford them indications of who or what the Originator of the universe may be; and have come to regard with mistrust, as wholly unreliable bases of argument, those moral and religious phenomena of their own and other men's souls, which may, after all, they hold, be only the results of the "set of the brain," determined by the accidents of their ancestors' condition, — "psychical habits" conveyed by hereditary transmission, but having no validity whatever as indicators of any external reality.

Now, even in the first of these stages, where we only interrogate Nature to confirm the yet undimmed faith of our hearts, there comes undoubtedly to us a chill when she returns her stammering reply, instead of the loud and glad response which we had been taught by the shallow old natural theology to expect with confidence. Instead of the "one chorus" which "all being" should, as we trusted, raise to the Maker of all, we hear an inarticulate mingling of psalms of joy with funeral dirges, the morning song of the bird with the death-cry of the hunted brute, the merry hum of the bee in the rose with the shrivelling of the moth in its "fruitless fire." Nature's incense rises one hour in balm and perfume to the skies, and the next steals along the ground, foul with the smell of blood and corruption.

We cannot shut out these things from our thought by any effort. We climb the mountains, where the "empty sky, the world of heather," seem all full of God; and we find beside the warbling brook a harmless sheep dying in misery, and its little lamb plaining and starving beside it. We wander through the holy cloisters of the woods till we have forgotten the world's sin and toil, and the scattered feathers and mangled breast of some sweet bird lie in our path, desecrating all the forest. We turn to the books which in former years used to expound to us the marvellous and beneficent mechanism of the Almighty Anatomist, and we grow sick as we read of the worse than devilish cruelties whereby Science has purchased her evermore unholy secrets. Further on, when we seek to reconcile the responses of the religious sentiment with those of the nature "red in tooth and claw," who shrieks against our creed, that love is "creation's final law," and treat them as two equally valid sources of knowledge, the riddle grows yet more terrible, till at last, when we discard the inward testimony to the Maker's character as unreliable, and look to the external world alone to tell us what he may be, we obtain the heart-chilling reply which Mr. Mill has left us as his last sad word, "A Mind whose power over the materials was not absolute, whose love for his creatures was not his sole actuating inducement, but who, nevertheless, desired their good."[1] "The scheme of Nature, regarded in its whole extent, cannot have had for its sole or even principal object the good of human or other sentient beings."[2] What is most disheartening is the reflection, that, to all appearance, this contradiction (real or apparent) between the inward voice of the soul and the voice of nature must not only continue, but become continually more clearly pronounced. There seems no chance at all that we shall ever find a better solution of any one of the "riddles of the painful earth" than we possessed before science set them in array; and, on the other hand, there is every reason to believe, that year by year, as the human conscience grows more enlightened, and sympathy with every form of suffering becomes stronger and more universal,

[1] Essays on Religion, p. 243. [2] Ibid., p. 65.

the pain conveyed to us by the sight of pain will become more acute, and our revolt at the seeming injustices of Providence consequently more agonizing.

In the second essay in this little book, I have endeavored to show, that, historically, we may trace an enormous and hitherto little suspected development in the social sentiment of man; and that, to judge from irresistible analogy, every future generation will have a livelier sympathy with the joys and sorrows of all sentient beings, such as, scarcely in their tenderest hours, the most loving souls of former ages experienced. This is, I conceive, the great hope for the future of humanity on earth, as the immortal life of love is, I believe, that of each human soul after passing through the portals of the grave. But with this fresh growth of sympathy has already come upon us quite a new sense of the vast extent, and the terrible depth, of the sufferings and wrongs existing around us; and the easy complacency wherewith our fathers regarded many of them, and the thanksgivings they returned for being "given more" than others, while conscious they did not deserve it, are well-nigh disgusting to us. Especially the sufferings of animals torture us, seen in the light of our new knowledge of their kindred sensibilities; and we stand aghâst before the long panorama of misery unrolled before us by the theory of the struggle for existence and the survival of the fittest at the expense of the unfit.

Much of the scepticism of the present day — so grave, so regretful, combined so often with the noblest philanthropy — is, beyond a doubt, the result of nothing else than the rapid growth of tenderer sentiments of compassion for unmerited suffering, and livelier indignation at suspected injustice. And, if this be so, future generations, as they become more just and more merciful, will also become more sceptical, — nay, more atheistic, — unless some different method be found for treating the dread difficulty than any of those which have been tried, and have broken down. Even for us now there is nothing more futile and disastrous than the attempt, either to treat doubt as "devil-born," instead of springing from that which is most divine in us, or to silence it, like the dog of hell, with a few handfuls of dry dust of commonplace. The man to whom the fact of the evil of the world first comes home in the hour of trial, and to whom are presented as explanations the platitudes in ordinary use by divines, is like one of those hapless persons of whom we heard not long ago, who stood waiting at the upper window of a burning house for means of escape: and, when the ladder was lifted, the brittle toy collapsed, and shivered in fragments on the pavement; and, with a never-to-be-forgotten cry of despair, the victims fell back into the fiery gulf behind them, and were seen no more.

How, then, ought the dread mystery of the existence of evil in creation to be treated? Historically, since men were far enough advanced to find that it is a problem, and to feel the incongruity in the alternate beneficence and severity of the unseen powers, which they had before contentedly supposed to be wayward and passionate as themselves, it has been explained in many different ways: 1st, By the Judaic, Greek, and Christian doctrine of a fall, succeeding to a golden, or Saturnian age of innocence and happiness; 2d, By the Zoroastrian, Egyptian, and Manichæan hypotheses of an Ahriman, or Typhon (evil principles, the rival of Ormuzd and Osiris), and the Hebrew doctrine of a Satan subordinate to Jehovah, but permitted to work mischief in his creation; 3d, By the Gnostic hypothesis of the intractable properties of Hylé (matter), wherewith the demiurge often contends ineffectually; 4th, By the orthodox Catholic doctrine, which, in addition to the fall and Satan, refers evil to the necessity for the presence of pain in a world intended to be one of trial; 5th, By the doctrine of Leibnitz (and substantially, also, that of Archbishop King), that the world is as good as it was possible to make it, every contingency other than those which it actually presents involving either greater evils or insuperable contradictions; 6th, By the doctrine of Theodore Parker, which is simply the vehement affirmation, on *à priori* grounds, that, in the creation of a God all-good and omnipotent, evil *must* be illusory, and a mere needful step to the highest good for every creature; lastly, By the doctrine, often timidly approached by previous thinkers, but for the first time, I believe, frankly stated by Mr. Mill, that, supposing God to be in any sense good, his character and dealings are explicable only on the hypothesis that he is possessed of very limited power and wisdom.

Such are the largest waves of human thought, which for countless ages have dashed themselves against this cloud-clapped rock. For us, in our day, few of them bear much significance: none can be said to be wholly satisfactory.

To explain natural evil and injustice by postulating the enormous injustice of punishing the whole human and animal creation for the sin of Adam would be held absurd, even had not geology superabundantly demonstrated the existence of the greatest natural evils before man, or even before the order of mammalia, came into being.

The hypothesis of a great bad God, whose opposition mars perpetually the work of the good Creator, though even yet accepted by a few minds of high philosophic cast, seems to the majority of us only to darken the dark mystery. The God who could create a Satan would be himself a Satan; and an uncreated Ahrimanes issuing out of "time without bounds" would be in morals what a circular triangle would be in mathematics — a self-contradiction. When we have postulated eternal existence, wisdom, and power, we have, *by our definition*, excluded malevolence, cruelty, and injustice.[1]

The "intractable properties of matter" may possibly indicate a class of causes which may stand for much in the solution of the riddle of evil; but till we have arrived at some conception of how the law of evolution is worked by the Lawgiver, and find the equivalent in modern scientific terminology for the earlier "creation" and the later "contrivance," it is little better than cheating ourselves with words, to speak of matter as either "intractable" or otherwise in the hands of God. When all is said, we are not far yet beyond the philosophy which taught, that

> "All are but parts of one stupendous whole,
> Whose body Nature is, and God the soul;"

and till we have learned something of the relation of our own bodies to our souls, of the "flesh" to the "spirit" against which it so often wars, it is hopeless to speculate on that of the material universe to its directing Mind. Certainly there is nothing in the visible world corroborating the notion of yet incomplete conquests of the demiurge over matter. No discoverer has found an outlying tract of chaos, any more than the "print of Satan's hoof in the

1 The notion of an absolutely evil principle is an express contradiction; for, as the principle resists the Good One, it also must be independent and infinite. But the notion of a Being infinitely evil is of one infinitely imperfect. Its knowledge and power, therefore, must be absolute ignorance and impotence." — LAW'S *Notes to King's Origin of Evil*

old red sandstone," the marks of the handiwork of any second or opposing intelligence. If Nature explains herself to us,

> "'Tis thus at the roaring loom of Time I ply,
> And weave for God the garb thou seest him by,"

that "garb" we behold is neither unfinished in the minutest hem, nor yet torn or spotted anywhere as by an enemy's hand. The red threads which run through it are woven into its very texture; nor is it possible to guess how some of them can ever be eliminated. Only the poet looks for the day when the "lion shall eat straw like the ox." The zoölogist knows, that, by the law of his being, the lion must prey on the lamb while the lamb and he inhabit together the earth. The "Holy Mountain," whereon they shall not "kill nor destroy," and where man and brute, and bird and insect, may live in peace and love, is, like heaven itself, unmarked in the chart of any geographer.

Again: the orthodox Catholic doctrine — that evil is necessary to afford scope for the moral freedom of man — is, I believe, valid as the explanation of a very large class of phenomena wherein man is principally concerned; but it is obvious that it leaves untouched the still harder problem of the misery of the brutes, since morals and geology have alike advanced too far to accept the theory which formerly supplemented it, that the "whole creation groaneth and travaileth in pain" for Adam's offence.

Again: the doctrine of Leibnitz — that it is the best of all worlds which could have been created — though, perhaps, nearer the truth than any other, must rather be deemed a statement of the problem than its solution, since he offers no suggestion as to the nature of that *necessity for not making it better*, which he is everywhere forced to assume as paramount to the divine benevolent Will.[1]

The unhesitating faith of Theodore Parker is one which few of us can regard without envy; and the mighty force of conviction with which he gave it utterance has served to warm and cheer a thousand hearts. God had revealed his absolute goodness in the very core of that large and loving heart; and, in the blaze of that divine light, he ceased to discern the darkness around. The result is, that he has contributed more than perhaps any other man of our age to kindle amongst us a fervent and fearless love towards God, which may help us, as it helped him, to say, "Though he slay me" — ay, and far worse, slay in my sight those who have never sinned as I

[1] Archbishop King, at the conclusion of his celebrated Treatise, — containing some valuable observations, and some singularly *naïf* examples of the circular mode of argument, — sums up his conclusions with much complacency thus: "The difficult question, then, 'Whence came evil?' is not unanswerable. It arises from the very nature and constitution of created beings, and could not be avoided without a contradiction. Though we are not able to apply these principles to all cases, we are sure they may be so applied" (Treatise on the Origin of Evil, 4th edit. p. 145). I wish I could share the archbishop's plenary satisfaction in the results of his labors.

have done — yet even so, "yet I will trust in him." But he has only provoked from the scientific side a somewhat contemptuous rejection of his dogmatic optimism, as making no real attempt to grapple with the difficulty of evil, or recognize its extent.[1]

Lastly: there remains the door of escape which Mr. Mill has set ajar, — the hypothesis that God, though benevolent, may be weak and ignorant, unable to do better than he has done for his creatures, albeit *that* is bad enough.[2] This theory I must here dwell upon for a few moments, both because it will, no doubt, for some time to come hold considerable place in men's thoughts, and also because it very importantly touches the chief purport of this book, — our hopes of the life after death. If God be really so feeble a being as Mr. Mill suggests, if his contrivances be so "clumsy" (p. 30), and even his own immortality open to doubt (p. 243), it is idle to argue any further concerning his goodness; for he may be sincerely desirous of giving to us eternal joy hereafter, and yet fail to do so as completely as he has failed to give us perfect

[1] It is evident from his biographies, that, in his earlier years, Theodore Parker was very deeply impressed by the sufferings of animals, and much disturbed thereby. What was the key by which he escaped out of Doubting Castle, I have never been able to ascertain.

[2] "And, since the exertion of all his power to make it as little imperfect as possible leaves it no better than it is, they cannot but regard that power, though vastly beyond human estimate, yet as in itself not merely finite, but *extremely limited.*" — *Essays on Religion*, p. 40.

happiness here. This world being the bungle it is reported to be, it is hopeless to count on what the sequel of it may prove.

If God's wisdom be really "limited," and his contrivances "clumsy," there is in Nature a very singular anomaly; for it appears that he has made a being more clever than himself, and able to point out where he has failed, if not exactly how to do better. The intelligence of man is the highest work of God with which we are acquainted (though nothing hinders us from supposing he may have made indefinitely nobler intelligent inhabitants of other worlds); but to suppose that this *chef d'œuvre* of the human brain is endowed with such similar but superior powers to its Maker as to be qualified to criticise and discriminate the clever from the clumsy among them, would be astonishing indeed. I do not mean this remark in the sense of the "brow-beating" of the human intellect to which divines are so prone. There can be no audacity in exercising any faculties with which we are gifted. I only desire to observe that there is, on the face of the matter, something very like absurdity in supposing that we, who on the hypothesis are ourselves God's handiwork, could find the end of his knowledge or wisdom. Practically, when we reflect on any one branch of the divine art, — on the architecture of the starry heavens, on the chemistry of the ever-shifting gases and fluids and solids in which creation every hour is born and dies, on the mechanism of the frame of an animalcule, or of our own bodies, say, of the hand alone, as exemplified in Sir Charles Bell's splendid treatise, — it seems indeed monstrous for us to open our lips regarding the wisdom of the Creator.

Where the limits of his power may lie is another question, of which it seems impossible we should ever guess the answer. Undoubtedly Christian theologians have written much folly about "Omnipotence;" having first invented a purely metaphysical term, and then argued back from it to facts, as if it were a specific datum within our measurement, like the horse-power of a steam-engine or an hydraulic-press. A more sober and reverent mode of regarding the stupendous Power above us may, as I have long hoped and argued, become a "note" of theism; and, in the full admission that there must be *some* limits even to supreme might (limits existing in the very nature of things, which cannot at once be, and not be, or unite contradictory properties, such as those of a circle and a triangle), we may find some help in contemplating such evils as those which seem to follow inevitably on the grant of moral freedom to a finite being such as man.

But such limitations of the divine Power as Mr. Mill seems to contemplate would narrow it (if I understand him rightly) far beyond this mere negation of contradictions; and, if we are to admit them into our philosophy, it ought surely to be on the ground that there are marks of such limits in

Nature, — places where the creative energy seems to have fallen short, or the obvious design has aborted. Now, it is possible that some evils in Nature — some forms of disease, for example — may seem to possess this character; but unquestionably the greater mass of evil bears no such marks. It is, as I have just said, woven into the very tissue of life on the planet, and seems just as much a part of the great plan as all the rest. All the terrible things in the world — the ruthless beak, the poisoned fang, the rending claw — are as much an integral part of the work as the downy breast of the bird, or the milk of the mother-brute. Further: there is a very curious parallel, which I do not think has received sufficient attention, between the exceptional *ugliness* in a beautiful world and the exceptional *evil* in a Good one, which, apparently, alike demand some other solution than that of a limitation of the Maker's power. The Creator has covered the earth, and filled the waters, with beauty. Almost every animal and shell, every tree and flower and seaweed, the mountains, the rivers, the oceans, every phase of day and night, summer and winter, is essentially beautiful. Our sense of beauty seems to be, not so much a beneficent adaptation to our dwelling-place (like our sense of taste for our food), but rather a filial sympathy with our great Father's pleasure in his own lovely creation, — a pleasure which he must have enjoyed millions of years before our race existed, when all the exquisite forms of animal and vegetable life filled the ancient lands and seas of the earliest geologic epochs. Nothing but a preference for beauty, for grace of form, and varied and harmonious coloring, inherent in the Author of the cosmos, can explain how it comes to pass that Nature is, on the whole, so refulgent with loveliness. But even here there are exceptions. Putting aside all man's monstrosities (and the beings who could create the Black Country might be counted by a dweller in the planet Mars as the brood of Ahrimanes), there are in the animal and the vegetable kingdom objects which are, strictly speaking, as *ugly* as the vast majority are beautiful. The same principle which authorizes us to pronounce an antelope or a Himalayan pheasant graceful and beautiful requires us to admit that the form of a rhinoceros is clumsy, and the colors of a macaw harsh and grating. If the song of the nightingale to its mate be musical, that of a peacock is frightful; and, if a firefly ranging among the roses of a southern night be a dream of beauty, a hairy and bloated tarantula spider hanging on the tree beside it causes us to shudder at its hideousness. Even amidst the flowers, which seem like love-gifts from heaven to man, there are, now and then, to be found some evil-looking, crawling, blotched, and sickly-smelling things, not to speak of those cruel and gluttonous Dionæa, which, by the irony of fate, have been brought so specially to our notice at this moment, as if, even in the study of the lilies of the field, we could no more be sure of finding comfort and rest of heart. Now, all these *uglinesses* in Nature are, I submit, real analogies to the sufferings of sentient creatures. They are few enough to be distinctly exceptional, but yet great and many enough, and bound up so completely in the chain of things, as to leave us no choice but to accept them as holding the same relation to the Author of Nature as all the rest.

What view can we take, then, of this mystery of ugliness, since it would seem that any hypothesis which may account for it may very possibly fit that yet greater and more dreadful mystery of suffering? Putting it thus before us, it seems absurd to say that perhaps the divine power was not equal to the task of harmonizing the macaw's color, or the peacock's voice, or of reducing to proportion and grace the unwieldy rhinoceros or the revolting spider. That his power should act freely in constructing the lion and the horse, the eagle and the ibis, the lark and the butterfly, and yet should be unaccountably thwarted and trammelled when he made the animals so strangely contrasted with them, is almost ridiculous to suppose. It seems, then, as impossible to frame an hypothesis which shall fit this æsthetic anomaly of Nature, as one which shall meet the moral anomaly of pain.

Thus, in short, it appears that every one of the theories on the origin of evil which have been put forth from the days of the Pentateuch to the appearance of these Essays on Religion, are more or less unsatisfactory and incomplete; and we may, with only too great probability, resign the hope that we shall ever hear of a better, or that any Œdipus will arise in the ages to come to resolve "the riddle of the painful earth," and relieve us from its direful pressure.

Two things only, I conceive, remain for us to do in the matter. The first is, to define somewhat more closely than, while oppressed by the declamations of pessimists, we are generally able to do, *what it is* in Nature which the human moral sense recognizes as evil. Secondly, to convince ourselves what is the testimony to the goodness of the Creator to be set over against it, which may enable us, not by any means to honor him on the balance, but to give him our heart-whole love and allegiance, and treat the mystery of evil as we should treat the inexplicable conduct of a revered father.

Of course, no attempt to accomplish adequately either of these purposes can be made in these pages. I shall only shortly indicate the character of the conclusions to which, in each case, I have myself arrived.

The first thing to be done, if we desire to define what we mean by evil, is to determine what we are justified in expecting as good, and then ask, What is there lacking of such good in the universe as we actually behold it? There is a principle which has been often laid down by sceptics, as if it were a self-evident axiom, but which appears to me to be nothing short of a monstrous misstatement. They affirm, that the existence of evil for an hour in the realm of a beneficent deity is just as inexplicable as the final triumph of evil to all eternity; and consequently, that where we find so much evil as prevails on earth, it is wholly impossible to say what extent and duration, even to infinity, may not be permitted to evil in other worlds, present or future.

This argument, I contend, is wholly fallacious. It turns on two false assumptions, — first, the perverse ascription to God of an omnipotence involving contradictions (e.g., that a creature could be made virtuous in a world devoid of trials); and, secondly, the application of the limitations of time proper to a weak and ignorant being such as man, to a being who is in certain possession of the power to carry out his purposes whenever he sees fit. The justice and goodness of God must, indeed, be the same as the justice and goodness of man: such is the cardinal postulate of all sound theology. But it does not follow, because man is bound to do justice and mercy *at once*, when the opportunity is presented to him (since he never knows whether it may come again), that God is similarly morally bound to rectify immediately every wrong, and relieve every pang. On the contrary, it seems clear, that, to an eternal and all-foreseeing Being, this principle of human ethics has no application, and that he rightly says to man,

"Tu n'as qu'un jour pour être juste
J'ai l'eternité devant Moi."

Even human parents are authorized to inflict pain, surgical or penal, which they reasonably believe to be calculated to benefit their children; and it is obvious that the rights of the divine Father, whose resources of compensation are infinite, must extend in this direction far beyond the bounds of the earthly horizon. All this line of argument, then, as against the divine justice, I consider to be wholly invalid. The point at which the human sense of justice as regards the relations of the Creator to the creature (a sense which I humbly believe God himself has planted in us, and authorized us to exercise) actually pronounces itself, is far different. We feel that it would be unjust to create a being *the sum of whose existence should be evil*, who endured, on the whole, more misery than he enjoyed happiness. And this, I maintain, holds good, even if the moral ill-deserts of that being should appear to merit overwhelming retributive punishment. The cruelest of all injustices would be to create a being, so constituted, and placed in such conditions, as that it should *in any way* come about that he should sink, not only into such misery, but such sin as should finally turn the scale, and make his whole existence a curse. Evil cannot be fitly predicated of any amount of suffering within these bounds, as if it were inconsistent with the divine justice; and all that the goodness of God leads us to expect is, that no suffering, small or great, should ever be meaningless and unnecessary, but that it should either have been inevitable as the condition of larger good, and in the maintenance of that eternal order in whose fixed warp the woof of our freedom alone can play; or else corrective and purgatorial, at once just, and in the highest sense merciful.

Taking our stand at this point, what is there that we must define as evil in the world? The outlook is threefold, and the answers correspondingly various. Has God been just and good to *us?* Has he been so to other men? Has he been so to the brutes? Most frequently men confound all these questions; and the answer which they find for the first determines that which they adopt for the second and the third; and thus the optimism of the prosperous, and the pessimism of the disappointed, may be readily explained. But though the dealings of God with each of us, as known to ourselves alone, may, and indeed do, serve us as presumptive evidence of the character of his dealings with others, it is plain it can be only on condition that we read them in their true moral significance. Mr. Morley has expressed somewhere his unmitigated disgust at those who are ready to proclaim that God is very good, because their lot happens to be a fortunate one, regardless of the misery of their fellows. But it is surely no less disgusting to find others denounce him as cruel and unjust, because (albeit he has treated them with infinite forbearance) he has left them to suffer some of the consequences of their errors; or because, in bestowing ninety-nine precious gifts, he has withheld the hundredth for which they crave? Here we come to one of many illustrations of the fact that the spiritual element in us alone enables us to judge truly of spiritual things. Spiritual men, without exception, testify, that, to their experience, God has been tenfold better than their deserts, more kind, more long-suffering, more infinitely father-like and merciful. Enduring every kind of loss, pain, or disappointment, their testimony is always the same; and, however much their faith is tortured by the evils they witness around them, it has never so much as occurred to them to think that God might have been better to themselves personally than he has actually been. It is reserved for quite another order of minds to express indignation, and a sense of injustice as regards their own destinies, and to argue that God has not (as Marcus Aurelius said) "done well for me and for the world;" that he ought to have given them their heart's desire, — health, wealth, or success; and that they have a right to complain of his dealings. What is the secret of this difference? It is, very simply, that the spiritual man has learned somewhat of what God is, and, correspondingly, of what he is himself, — the one so good and holy, that the very thought of injustice cannot be directed towards him after the experience of his forgiving love; the other so sinful, so vacillating, so ungrateful, that his never-ending wonder is, how God continues to him the least of his mercies. Very possibly, among the chief of God's kindnesses he may reckon some acute suffering of body or mind which has driven him back from the ways of worldliness and sin, and restored him to his better self. Thus, then, to the question, "Has God been good and just to us individually?" it will be found, I think, that different answers will generally be given by religious and irreligious men. The first never think themselves to have deserved so much good as they have received: the second rarely think themselves to have deserved so much evil.

On first noticing this fact, the natural corollary seems to be, that in the life of every man, could we read it similarly *from the inside*, we should likewise trace the same contrast. But the rule cannot hold good as regards the tens of thousands who have never known any thing deserving the name of a religion; whose natures have been crushed, warped, stunted from childhood, or trampled down in manhood or womanhood, into the mire of vice and shame, instead of being lifted into spirituality; nor yet of the millions of innocent children who have suffered and died in infancy. Some difference will appear in the *incidence* of the preponderance of evil in the moral or in the physical life, according as we regard happiness as the end and aim of existence, or believe that end to consist in virtue, and eternal union with God. But in either case (as I have argued at length in the succeeding essay), it is certain that the mass of mankind neither attain to such degree of happiness nor of virtue as that we can pronounce it to be positively "good," or to any which excludes very considerable evil.

Even here, however, regarding this great amount of evil in human life, we must guard ourselves against exaggeration, and especially against the fallacy of treating it as if it ever, or anywhere, *outbalanced* good. Where evil passions should actually preponderate over innocent or virtuous propensities, society must fall asunder, and human affairs come to a standstill; and where want and pain should prevail over satisfied appetite and ease, mortal life must terminate. In these days we need to be reminded again of the once familiar observation, that "it is a happy world, after all;" that all our senses normally convey pleasure, not pain; and that the exercise of the faculties of heart and brain and limbs are all (under their proper conditions) delightful. We remark on a case of destitution, or on a friend's bodily suffering or bereavement; but we could not find tongue to tell of all those around us who have sufficient food and clothing, who are free from pain, and who enjoy the sweet happiness of home affections. Many of us live for months and years without pain; but few live a day without pleasure, if it be only the pleasure of food and sleep, and of intercourse with their kind.

And again: it ought to be borne in mind, as setting limits to our notions of evil, that it has diminished, in a perceptible degree, in successive ages. Perhaps this lessening is not so great as we once fondly imagined, and that the progress of mankind is far from being achieved without drawbacks: still it would appear there are decidedly more and higher pleasures now enjoyed, and fewer and lesser pains now suffered, by mankind, than in any preceding age of the world.

Here, then, rest our conclusions regarding evil in human existence. It is vast; and much of it is wholly inexplicable by any of the hypotheses which have passed current as its explanation. But, great as it is, the good in human life is greater still, and shows a constant tendency to gain ground upon it.

Regarding the suffering of animals, it seems, that, if our fathers treated it much too lightly in their sublime contempt for the brutes, we are not exempt from the danger of taking too dark a view of it. Mr. Mill says, for example,[1] that "if a tenth part of the pains which have been expended in finding beneficent adaptations in all Nature had been employed in collecting evidence to blacken the character of the Creator, what scope for comment would not have been found in the entire existence of the lower animals, divided, with scarcely an exception, into devourers and devoured, and a prey to a thousand ills from which they are denied the faculties

[1] Nature, p. 58.

necessary to protect themselves!" I cannot but protest against words like these, as quite equally misleading with the easy-going optimism of Paley and his congeners. The lives of the lower animals, so far as we can understand their consciousness, are *not*, on the whole, a pain, but a pleasure. When undisturbed by human cruelty, they suffer but little, or rarely till the closing scene; and though that is, alas! too often one of anguish, it scarcely occupies, in any case, a hundredth or a thousandth part of their existence. In the interval of days, months, or years, between birth and death, they have evidently much ease, and not a little delight. They enjoy the gambols of youth, undimmed by the pains of human education; the passion of love, unchecked by shame or disappointment; the perpetually recurring pleasures of food, rest, and exercise; and (in the case of the female birds and brutes) the exquisite enjoyments of their tender motherhood. The sum and substance of their lives under all normal conditions is surely beyond question happy, and the anxieties and cares which in their position would be ours, and which we are apt to lend them in imagination, are by them as totally unfelt as are our miserable vanities, our sorrowful memories, and our bitter remorse. The scene which the woods and pastures present to a thoughtful eye of a summer morning is not one to "blacken" the character of the Creator, but to lift up the soul in rapture, and prompt us to add a human voice of thanksgiving to the chirp of the happy birds, the bleating of the playful lambs, and the hum of the bees in the cowslips and the clover.

The law by which the death of one animal is needful to the life of another is undoubtedly one whose working it is impossible for us to contemplate without pain. The process of killing and devouring, if, on the whole, less productive of suffering than the slow death of age and want, is yet, in millions of cases, accompanied by circumstances horrible to think of. Nor is it at all evident why natural death should not itself have been made painless, rather than that recourse should have been had to such an alternative. Obviously, if creatures had not been made to devour one another, scarcely a hundredth part of those which now throng the earth and waters could have existed; and each individual may be said to hold his life on the tenure of relinquishing it when summoned for another's support.[1] Still the law is undoubtedly, to our sense, a harsh one; and when we add to its action the sufferings of animals from disease, from noxious insects and parasites, from cold, from hunger, and, above all, from the cruelty of man,[2] we have undoubtedly accumulated

1 Archbishop King says, "God could have created an inanimate machine which should have supplied animals with food. But a being that has life is preferable to one that has not. God, therefore, animated that machine which furnishes out provision for the more perfect animals." — *Origin of Evil*, c. iii. § 5.

2 It is probable that every harmless little calf killed by the vile old process for producing white veal suffers as much as a crucified man.

a mass of evil very awful to contemplate. But it is wrong to exaggerate even here, or speak as if the lives of the brutes were, on the whole, a curse, and not a blessing. Even we, who in our cruelty so often seek them only to hurt and destroy, yet see them — bird, beast, and insect — ninety-nine times out of a hundred, happy, and enjoying themselves, for once we notice them in any kind of pain. The same rule applies to our impressions as in the case of human suffering. We are so much more struck by the sight of pain than of ordinary pleasure and well-being, that we carry away a vivid impression of the former, and forget the latter.

Brought to its actual limits, then, I conceive the problem of evil stands before us as a vast, but not an *immense*, exception in a rule of good. A certain large share of it we can recognize as having great moral purposes fully justifying its existence, and even elevating it into the rank of beneficence. Such are the sufferings (of rational beings) which punish and repress sin, and those through whose fires the noblest and the purest virtues have ever passed to perfection. That there is some wondrous power in suffering thus to bring out of human souls qualities immeasurably nobler than are ever developed without its aid is a fact equally plain to those who have watched the almost divine transformation it sometimes effects upon characters hitherto hard, selfish, or commonplace ; and to those who have noted how thin-natured and unsympathetic if not selfish, are at the best, those men and women who have lived from youth to age in the unbroken sunshine of prosperity. Even among very ordinary characters, and where the lesson of suffering has not been deep, there are very few of us, I believe, who, after the lapse of a little while, would wish that we could unlearn it, or return to be the slighter, feebler, shallower-hearted beings we were before it came. Rather do we recognize the truth of the poet's words : —

> "The energies too stern for mirth,
> The reach of thought, the strength of will,
> 'Mid cloud and tempest have their birth;
> Through blight and blast their course fulfil."

Another share of evil may be attributed to, though not altogether explained by, the beneficent purpose of securing preponderating physical advantage to the sufferer ; as, for example, the pains which guard the integrity of the bodies of animals. But, beyond all these, we are compelled mournfully to conclude that there exists, both in human life and in the life of the brutes, a large mass of evil, which can by no such hypotheses be accounted for consistently with the benevolence of the Creator, and which utterly baffles now, and will probably forever baffle, the ingenuity of mortal man so to explain.

What is it that shall help us to look this great residuum of inexplicable evil in the face? Where shall we find ground of faith whereon we may take our stand, and confront it with unshaken hearts?

Strange it is indeed to say, that I have hopes that the publication of the Essays on Nature, the Utility of Religion and Theism, which will give such bitter pain to all believing hearts, such double sadness to those who, like myself, regard their author with undying honor and gratitude, may even prove the turning-point of this controversy, may set us at last on the right track for the solution of the problem. For what have we in these powerful, limpidly clear, bravely outspoken words? We have, for the first time perhaps in human history, revealed sharply and distinctly what that element in human nature must be, which, to the majority of mankind, is the origin and organ of religion, and which it is so transparently evident that Mr. Mill *had not.*[1] Hitherto we

[1] Let it be understood, that, in speaking of the religious sentiment as deficient in Mr. Mill's nature, I use the term expressly in the sense of *that spiritual organ whereby man obtains direct perception of the living God.* In the broader meaning of the word, implying general reverence and tenderness towards all things noble and holy, — a sense of the mystery surrounding human life, and a fervent devotion to the ideal of duty, — Mr. Mill was assuredly an eminently religious man. How it came to pass that such a soul could by any mortal hand be debarred from the happiness of direct recognition of God, is one of the riddles wherewith the spiritual as well as the physical world is full. As he himself says, "It is possible to starve an instinct;" and, as Mr. Upton has well explained in his profound paper on the "Experience-Philosophy and Religious Belief," beside all other conditions on which spiritual knowledge is obtained, it is needful "that the understanding should be freed from all tyrannous misconceptions which preclude or distort the intellectual cognizance of spiritual truth." Nothing short of such a divine *blow* as smote

have seen it in its highest development in the saints, and had opportunity to learn what it *positively* is. But so natural does it seem to man, so much does it, in ordinary men and women, harmonize with and shade off into the moral, affectional, and ratiocinative faculties, that it was easy to mistake their action for its own. Now it seems possible to learn more of it by the aid of the complete self-revelation of a very noble mind, wherein, owing to almost unique circumstances, the whole element has been eliminated; and we are left to mark what are the tracts of human nature which it normally covers, and which are found to lie bare, like the seashore when that mighty tide has flowed away back to its bed. We behold one of the keenest intellects of this or any century, and, on the human side, one of the tenderest and most capacious of hearts; a man whose moral sense (whatever were his theories of its nature) quivered with intensest life, and was true as needle to the pole of the loftiest justice to man, to woman, and to brute, who yet, great philosopher as he was, when he comes to deal with a subject on which the rude tinker of Bedford has instructed the world, writes like a blind man discoursing of colors,

St. Paul would have been strong enough to overthrow the "tyrannous misconceptions" wherewith Mr. Mill's education must have fenced his mind. I need scarcely add, that, in my view, the absence of *conscious recognition* of the relations between God and the soul is very far indeed from implying the non-existence of such relations, or the loss of some of the richest blessings which they bestow.

or a deaf man criticising the contortions of a violinist wasted on the delusion of music. When he speaks of the utility of religion, he confounds, as if they were identical, those realms of human nature which public opinion or human authority may sway, and those which, in the solemn hours of visitation from the Divine Spirit, fall under the inner law of conscience and of love. And, when he writes of the consciousness of God, all he has to say of it is to refer to the metaphysical subtleties of Cousin about the laws of perception, and to add contemptuously, —

> "It would be a waste of time to examine any of these theories in detail. While each has its particular logical fallacies, they labor under the common infirmity, that one man cannot, by proclaiming with ever so much confidence that *he* perceives an object, convince other people that they see it too. . . . When no claim is set up to any peculiar gift, but we are told that all of us are as capable as the prophet of seeing what he sees, feeling what he feels, nay, that we actually do so; and when the utmost effort of which we are capable fails to make us aware of what we are told we perceive, — this supposed universality of intuition is but
>
> 'The dark lantern of the spirit,
> Which none see by but those who bear it;'
>
> and the bearers may be asked to consider whether it is not more likely that they are mistaken as to the origin of an impression on their minds than that others are ignorant of the very existence of an impression on theirs." [1]

[1] P. 163.

The friends who can have told Mr. Mill that he saw, or was capable of seeing, religious truth as a Tauler or a Fénelon saw it, or of feeling on the subject as even much less religious men are accustomed to feel, were bold indeed. It may have been a hard task to say that such was not the case. Nobody could have ventured upon it during his life, or even after his death, had he not thrown down the challenge, and elaborately explained to us the way in which his religious instincts were destroyed by his ruthless father. But now the matter stands plain; and I confess I look with some confidence to the results of the act of the elder Mill in extirpating the organ of religion from his child's heart, as serving to reveal to us the place it naturally takes among human faculties. Even at the cost of all the desolation the book will spread around, it is, perhaps, well that this dreadful experiment should, once for all, have been tried, and not in any "vile body" of fool or egotist, but in the person of one of the ablest, and in all things beside one of the very noblest, of men.

That lesson, then, is this: that, as we did not first gain our knowledge of God from the external world, so we shall never obtain our truest and most reliable idea of him from the inductions which science may help us to draw from it. Spiritual things *must* be spiritually discerned, or we must be content. never to discern them truly at all. In man's soul alone, so far as we may yet discover, is the moral nature of his Maker revealed, as the sun is mirrored in a mountain lake. While all the woods and moors and pastures are quivering in its heat, we only behold the great orb reflected in the breast of that deep, solitary pool. If (as we must needs hold for truth) there be a moral purpose running through all the physical creation, its scope is too enormous, its intricacy too deep, the cycle of its revolution, like that of some great sidereal period, too immense, for our brief and blind observation. It must be enough for us to learn what God bids *us* to be of just and merciful and loving, and then judge what must be his justice, his mercy, and his love. That Being whom the sinful soul meets in the hour of its penitence, and the grateful heart in its plenitude of thanksgiving, and every man who really prays in the moments of supreme communion, — *that* God is One concerning whom the very attempt to *prove* that he is infinitely good seems almost sacrilege. It is *as* goodness, as holiness, love and pity ineffable, that he has revealed himself. Shall we treat all that we have so learned on our knees as idle self-delusions, and barricade with iron shutters the windows of the soul which look out heavenward, and this in the name of sense and reason? Nay; but let us fling those windows wide open, and again, and yet again, seek to renew the celestial vision. These sacred faculties of our nature have a right to their exercise, as well as those which tell us of the properties of solids, fluids, and gases, of light and electricity. Their reports may be false? So may be every thing we call knowledge, every report of the senses, every conclusion of the logical intellect. A persistent and widely recognized fact of human consciousness may be illusory; but there is no better proof to be had, even of the existence of an external world.[1]

1 An excellent illustration of this subject, expressing very closely my own view of it, is to be found in the following letter, published in the Spectator, Sept. 5, 1874: —

"Will you give me space for an illustration in support of that which, apart from revelation, is surely the best proof of all of the existence of God, — the existence, viz., of that religious instinct in man, which, on Prof. Tyndall's and Mr. H. Spencer's own scientific principles, should be the subjective response to some objective reality, — the adaptation of the creature man to his 'environment'? The dog has a religion, and his deity is man. Previous to the introduction of man upon the scene, the dog must have been simply dog, minus this quasi-religious faculty. But man appears, and makes his appeal to the dog-nature: in response, a capacity for human fellowship is developed in the dog, and is *inherited;* so that a craving for such fellowship becomes, thenceforth, part of his nature.

"Now, if we imagine some being, some detached intelligence, with power to observe the dog in his development through the ages, but to whom the man, on his introduction, is *invisible,* what a strange problem would present itself for his solution! Would not the higher development of the dog, as now observed by him, be analogous to the calling-forth of the religious instinct in the creature man? The observer would now see with wonder the frequent reference to a seemingly higher will, not always cheerfully yielded to. He would note the upward look, the overcoming of mere animal impulses, the occasional wilful outbreak of the lower nature, bringing with it a sense of guilt, to be followed by shame, penitence, and meek submission to chastisement; strangest thing of all, he would see this chastisement seemingly accepted as a medium of reconciliation with some invisible being, whereby peace and contentment are restored to the canine mind.

"Which would be the soundest conclusion for such an observer as I have supposed to come to, — that these phenomena of dog-conscious-

The great root passion of normally constituted humanity, the craving to find some One to whom to look up with absolute moral reverence, a passion, which, even within the last few months, the greatest thinkers on the agnostic side have one after another admitted to be a fundamental and ineradicable element in our nature, — that exalted aspiration can never find the smallest satisfaction in the notion of a probable God, who is probably more benevolent than otherwise. Mr. Mill arrives at the conclusion that such lights as we possess "afford no more than a preponderance of probability of the existence of a Creator, of his benevolence a considerably less preponderance; that there is some reason to think that he cares for the pleasure of his creatures, but by no means that this is his sole care, or that other purposes do not often take precedence of it."[1]

Further on, he grants that the "ideally perfect character . . . *may* have a real existence in a

ness were self-evolved, mere subjective illusions; or that, outside the range of his vision, there was some real object to call them forth? To the obvious criticism, that, as a matter of fact, the dog does apprehend man, his deity, by his senses, while man does not thus apprehend God, the reply is, that though, in many cases, it may be latent, there is in man a higher sense whereby, and that with an intense reality, the invisible God has been and is apprehended by countless thousands.

"Supposing the evolution theory to be true, the question arises, When did man, the thinking animal, become man the religious being? May not this example of a somewhat parallel phenomenon in a lower field supply an answer; viz., When his nature, however previously developed, was first consciously acted upon by a higher nature? I am, sir, &c., "HENRY F. BATHER."

[1] P. 208.

Being to whom we owe all such good as we enjoy."[1] But such an hypothesis can only be admitted on condition of supposing that "his power over his materials was not absolute;" that "his love for his creatures was not his sole actuating inducement;"[2] and, finally, that, even of his "continued existence," we have not a thoroughly satisfactory "guaranty."[3] But, as such a being as this is no God at all to the needs either of the conscience or of the heart, we are, consequently, not surprised to find Mr. Mill setting him aside in favor of that "standard of excellence," Jesus Christ. Here is another wonderful exemplification of the eminent presence of the moral, and the total absence of the spiritual, element in this great thinker. He perfectly recognized the moral beauty of Christ's character as transcribed by history; but his inward eye was closed to that supreme loveliness which is spiritually revealed to every soul which enters into communion with God, and which, shining full into the heart of Christ, made him the mirror wherein humanity has ever since seen it reflected.

The fact that we *want* a perfect God does not, of course, prove that any such Being exists; but it leaves such a Deity as Mr. Mill has propounded for our *quasi*-belief altogether outside the *religious* question. If the intellect or the fancy may be contented with a probable God, provisionally accepted as benevolent, it is certain that the religious senti-

[1] P. 253. [2] P. 243. [3] P. 243.

ment can no more attach itself to such a Deity than a man can embrace a cloud. A balance of probabilities may properly determine our choice of an investment for a sum of money; but, when it comes to the gift of our heart's allegiance, we need a different kind of assurance. No man can stand by patiently while arguments *pro* and *con* are carefully weighed, and begin to love when the scale turns by a hair on the side of benevolence, and drop on his knees in reverence as justice begins to preponderate, and adore when the balance of good appears finally by some degrees heavier than that of evil. If this be so, then it follows that the inductive method is forever inapplicable to the solution of the greater problems of theology, because, under the most favorable circumstances, it can only give us a balance of more or less probability, — a *general*, not a *universal* proposition. We are compelled to seek in some other modes of thought an assurance of quite another kind.

I am far from conceding that no more decisive witness to the divine Existence and Goodness than Mr. Mill has found in the external world is to be drawn therefrom strictly by the inductive method. Respecting God's existence, it seems to me the summary of arguments in Mr. Thornton's recent admirable treatise[1] leaves the scientific atheist a standing-room so infinitesimally small, that nothing

[1] Old-Fashioned Ethics, &c. See the chapter on Recent Phases of Scientific Atheism.

short of one of those angels of whom the rabbins taught that a legion may rest on the point of a needle could support himself thereon. And, regarding the divine moral character, I must protest against the unaccountable manner in which, when the experience-philosophy holds its court, the most important of the witnesses is rarely or ever put in the box. Why is it, I ask, that while every minute fact of organic and inorganic Nature is freely cited as bearing testimony more or less important to the character of the Creator, — why is the supreme fact, the existence of man, of a being who loves, and who prays, who has deep set within him the ideas of justice and of duty, a being capable of becoming a hero, a martyr, a saint, —why is this greatest of all the facts of Nature which our globe presents, passed over by the experimentalist with no notice at all so far as it bears on the theistic argument? Let us waive, for a moment, all question of personal intuitive or spiritual knowledge. Let us suppose that we, individually, have no such transcendental moral or religious knowledge, and that we are regarding the human race altogether *ab extra*. Even so, such "facts of experience" as an Isaiah, a Christ, a Buddha, a Plato, a Marcus Aurelius, certainly claim attention as much as any of the facts from which the Creator's indifference to his creatures' welfare, or incapacity to make them happy, has been inductively inferred. After all which has been said of recent years regarding the way in which our moral natures may be supposed to have been developed out of the instincts of the ape, there is nothing so wonderful in all the wide circuit of science as that it should happen, that in a world teeming with injustice, and in which Nature's "recklessness" is her prevailing characteristic,[1] there should exist a being whose brain has acquired such a "set" of passionate love for justice, as that, for its sake, he is often ready to sacrifice happiness and life.

And again: I think even the experience-philosophy, when its conclusions are reduced to logical coherency, points to the perfection of the moral attributes of the Supreme Being. Such a Being either has, or has not, a moral nature. If he *have* one, then he cannot be partially good or partially just, — half God, half Devil, — with a fickle or a checkered character. So much as this is involved in the hypothesis of a Creator transcending all the wants, pains, weaknesses, ignorances, and passions of the creature. If any preponderance of evidence in Nature, then, appears to show that God has moral purposes, and that those purposes are, in the majority of cases, benevolent, we are compelled, for mere coherency sake, to arrive *per saltum* at the conclusion, that, if he be good so far, he must be good altogether. On these grounds, then, even such a small residuum of the sublime idea of God as is left us by the rigid application of the experimental philosophy to theology may be made to harmonize

[1] Essays on Religion, p. 28.

with and corroborate the faith derived from a higher source of knowledge; and the Atheistic and *Kakotheistic* creeds stand condemned, even in the court of Nature.

But I repeat, that such arguments have in my eyes but little worth save as intellectual satisfactions; and I would as lief, for my own part, forego all such conclusions of my understanding regarding the Great Power who dwells behind the veil of Nature, if I could not find in my heart the Lord of life and love, our all-holy, all-merciful Father and God.

A few words must be added, in conclusion, respecting Mr. Mill's remarks on the doctrine with which this little book is directly concerned, — that of the immortality of the soul. After having described the reasons which he conceives have acted as powerful *causes of the belief*, not as rational *grounds* for it, and then stated the arguments deduced from the goodness of God, he observes: —

"These might be arguments in a world, the constitution of which made it possible, without contradiction, to hold it for the work of a Being at once omnipotent and benevolent; but they are not arguments in a world like that in which we live. . . . With regard to the supposed improbability of his having given the wish without its gratification, the same answer may be made. The scheme which either limitation of power, or conflict of purposes, compelled him to adopt, may have *required* that we should have the wish, although it were not destined to be gratified. . . . There is, therefore, no assurance whatever, of a life after death on grounds of natural religion. But to any one who feels it conducive, either to his satisfaction or his usefulness, to hope for a future state as a possibility, there is no hinderance to his indulging that hope. Appearances point to the existence of a Being who has great power over us, — all the power implied in the creation of the cosmos, or of its organized being, at least, — and of whose goodness we have evidence, though not of its being his predominant attribute; and, as we do not know the limits of either his power or his goodness, there is room to hope that both the one and the other may extend to granting us this gift, provided that it would be really beneficial to us." [1]

After having held before us this even balance of probabilities that we shall, or shall not, live again after death, Mr. Mill further discusses how far the indulgence of hope in a region of mere imagination ought to be encouraged, or discouraged, as a "departure from the rational principle of regulating our feelings, as well as opinions, strictly by evidence," and gives his verdict in favor of "making the most of any even small probabilities on this subject, which furnish imagination with any footing to support itself upon." [2] This observation, again, is followed up by many pertinent remarks on the benefits derivable from looking habitually to the brighter and nobler side of things; and, with regard to the prospect of immortality, he adds, that the benefit of the doctrine "consists less in any specific hope than in the enlargement of the general scale of the feelings," [3] and that it is "legitimate, and philosophi-

[1] Essays on Religion, pp. 209, 210. [2] P. 245. [3] P. 250.

cally defensible, while we recognize as a clear truth that we have no ground for more than a hope."

Now, to those amongst us who do not believe that great benefits are ever derived from crediting delusions, and who do not feel in themselves the inclination to cultivate and water a hope which they know to be a flower stuck rootless by a child in the ground, this kind of exhortation is as strange as that which follows it on the "infinitely precious familiarity of the imagination with the conception of a morally perfect Being;" the same idealization of our standard of excellence in a person "being quite possible even when that person is conceived as merely imaginary."[1] Meditating upon imaginary gods, and cherishing hopes which are known to depend on an even balance of probabilities, seems, to most of us, very like the mournful preservation of a casket when the jewel is stolen, of a cage when the bird is flown, forever reminding us of an irreparable loss. Far better, to our apprehensions, would it be to gather courage from our despair, and face as best we may the facts (if facts they be) that we have either no Father above, or that he is weak and unwise, and that our hopes beyond the grave hang on a straw, than mock these solemn trusts of the human soul in God and immortality by "making believe," like children, that we possess them when they are ours no more. "Si Dieu n'existait pas il faudrait l'inventer," is an epigram which has now

[1] Essays on Religion, p. 250.

been paralleled, "If we are not immortal, we had better think ourselves so." Yet there seems some contradiction in Mr. Mill's view of the advantages of the hope altogether. In the preceding essay on the Utility of Religion, he makes very light of it. He says, —

> "When mankind cease to need a future life as a consolation for the sufferings of the present, it will have lost its chief value to them for themselves. I am now speaking of the unselfish. Those who are so wrapped up in self, that they are unable to identify their feelings with any thing which will survive them require the notion of another selfish life beyond the grave to keep up any interest in existence." [1]

Here, again, surely we meet the singular train of misapprehensions which seem to crowd upon the writer from his incapacity to understand the religious sentiments of other men. It is precisely the selfish man who has had a comfortable life here below, who may inscribe on his tombstone that he

> "From Nature's temperate feast rose satisfied,
> Thanked Heaven that he had lived, and that he died,"

and made no demand for further existence for himself or anybody else. But the unselfish man, who has looked abroad with aching heart upon a sinful and suffering world cannot thus be content to rise with a sanctimonious grace from the feast of life (so richly spread for him), and to leave Lazarus starving at his doors. That his own life on earth

[1] P. 119.

should have been so happy, so replete with the joys of the senses, the intellect, and the affections; that he should have been kept from sinking into the slough of vice, and permitted to taste some of the unutterable joys of a loving and religious life, — all this makes it only the more inexplicable, and the more agonizing to him to behold his brothers and sisters — no worse, he is well assured, and often far better, than himself — dragging out lives of misery, and privation of all higher joy, and dying perhaps at last, so far as their own consciousness goes, in final alienation and revolt from God and goodness. It is for these that he *demands* another and a better life at the hands of the divine Justice and Love; and in as far as he loves both God and man, so far is he incapable of renouncing that demand, and resting satisfied because *he* has had a pleasant mortal existence, and because younger men will enjoy the like after him, and, when he is gone, help to "carry on the progressive movement of human affairs." The prayer of his soul, "Thy kingdom come," includes indefinitely more than this.

Further: the writer's lack of the religious sense is once more revealed by the absence of any reference, in the summary of the reasons why men hope for another life, to that which must always be to religious persons the supreme hope of all. Mr. Mill expresses, in a few most touching words (what he, of all men, could not have failed to know), how the sceptic loses one most valuable consolation, —

"the hope of re-union with those dear to him, who have ended their earthly life before him." "That loss," he adds, "is neither to be denied nor extenuated. In many cases, it must be beyond the reach of comparison or estimate, and will always suffice to keep alive in the more sensitive natures the imaginative hope of a futurity, which, if there is nothing to prove, there is as little in our knowledge or experience to contradict." These words will find an echo in every heart. There is no "extenuation" of the immeasurable loss of the hope of meeting once more with the beloved dead; and, when M. Comte sets forth the satisfaction of being buried by their side, — that we may *perish*, instead of *living*, together, — it would seem as if he meant to mock at the anguish of mortal bereavement, as some grim tyrant who has promised to release a captive, and fulfils his word by giving back his corpse. But has Mr. Mill, who so deeply understands what the longing for the re-union of *human* love may mean, never known the aspiration of every religious man for the communion of divine love in a world where we shall sin against it no more, and where it may be more perfectly unbroken than is possible while we stand behind the veil of the flesh? This longing desire, which lies at the very core of every God-loving heart, is surely worth mention among the reasons for hoping for immortality, even if it cannot be accepted, according to the principle of experimental philosophy, as ground for the faith that every son of God who has felt it is, even in right thereof, immortal.

But I quit the ungracious, and, in my case, most ungrateful, task of offering my feeble protest against the last words given to us of a man so good and great, that even his mistakes and deficiencies (as I needs must deem them) are more instructive to us than a million platitudes and truisms of teachers whom his transcendent intellectual honesty should put to the blush, and whose souls never kindled with a spark of the generous ardor for the welfare of his race which flamed in his noble heart, and animated his entire career.

In conclusion, while commending to the reader's consideration what appears to me the true method of solving the problem of a life after death, I have but to point out the fact, that on the answer to that great question must hang the alternative, not only of the hope or despair of the human race, but of the glory or the failure of the whole cosmos, so far as our uttermost vision can extend. Lions and eagles, oaks and roses, may be good after their kind; but if the summit and crown of the whole work, the being in whose consciousness it is all mirrored, be worse than incomplete and imperfect, an undeveloped monster, an acorn mouldered in its shell, a bud blighted by the frost, then must the entire world be deemed a failure also. Now, man can only be reckoned on any ground as a *provisionally* successful work, — successful, that is, provided we regard him as *in transitu*, on his way to another and far more perfect stage of development. We are content that the egg, the larva, the bud, the half-painted canvas, the rough scaffolding, should only faintly indicate what will be the future bird and butterfly and flower and picture and temple. And thus to look on man (as by some deep insight he has almost universally regarded himself) as a "sojourner upon earth," upon his way to "another country, even a heavenly," destined to complete his pilgrimage, and make up for all his shortcomings elsewhere, is to leave a margin for believing him to be even now a divine work in its embryonic stage. But if we close out this view of the future, and assure ourselves that nothing more is ever to be expected of him than what we knew him to be during the last days of his mortal life; if we are to believe we have seen the best development which his intellect and heart, his powers of knowing, feeling, enjoying, loving, blessing, and being blessed, will ever obtain while the heavens endure, — then, indeed, is the conclusion inevitable and final. Man is a failure, the consummate failure of creation. Every thing else — star, ocean, mountain, forest, bird, beast, and insect — has a sort of completeness and perfection. It is fitting in its own place; and it gives no hint that it ought to be other than it is. "Every lion," as Parker has said, "is a type of all lionhood; but there is no man who is a type of all manhood." Even the best and greatest of men have only been imperfect types of a single phase of manhood, — of the saint, the hero, the sage, the philanthropist, the poet, the friend, — never of the full-orbed man who should be all these together. If each perish at death, then, as the seeds of all these varied forms of good are in each, every one is cut off prematurely, blighted, spoiled. Nor is this criterion of success or failure solely applicable to our small planet, a mere spark thrown off the wheel whereon a million suns are turned into space. It is easy to believe that much loftier beings, possessed of far greater mental and moral powers than our own, inhabit other realms of immensity. But thought and love are, after all, the grandest things which any world can show; and if a whole race endowed with them proves such a failure as death-extinguished mankind would undoubtedly be, then there remains no reason why all the spheres of the universe should not be similar scenes of disappointment and frustration, and creation itself one huge blunder and mishap. In vain may the president of the British Congress of Science dazzle us with the splendid panorama of the material universe unrolling itself "from out of the primeval nebula's fiery cloud." Suns and planets swarming through the abysses of space are but whirling sepulchres, after all, if, while no grain of dust is shaken from off their rolling sides, the conscious souls of whom they have been the palaces are all forever lost. Spreading continents and flowing seas, soaring Alps and fertile plains, are worse than failures, if we, even we, poor, feeble, sinful, dim-eyed creatures that we are, shall ever "vanish like the streak of morning cloud in the infinite azure of the past."

For the concluding essay in this book, wherein I have endeavored to explain what I deem to be the best hope of the human race here on earth, I have to crave the reader's forgiveness for two defects, of which I am thoroughly sensible. One is, that I have attempted to compress the statement of a large and somewhat revolutionary theory of human development into a compass far too small to do justice to whatever claims it may have upon acceptance. Should the psychological fact, which I imagine myself to have for the first time brought to notice, provoke any discussion, I could readily double again and again the illustrations of it given in these brief pages; and, even since they were written, I may boast that they have received singular confirmation (so far as the story of the Aryan race is concerned) in the profound work of the Rev. George Cox.[1] It would, however, no doubt require a somewhat voluminous treatise dedicated to the purpose to establish thoroughly the principle for which I contend.

Secondly, I must ask (albeit I scarcely expect to receive) condonation for the presumption of offering a new word (*heteropathy*) to define the hitherto unnoticed sentiment to which I wish to direct attention. Between the inevitable result of causing

[1] History of Greece, vol. i. ch. ii.

every critic to make merry with the word, instead of seriously discussing the thing it signifies, and the opposite danger of leaving my argument logically floundering among terms none of which express accurately what I mean, I have chosen the former alternative, and must, of course, suffer the consequences, against which, however, I now put forth this plea in mitigation. Persons who feel any genuine interest in a somewhat curious, if not really a novel or valuable, psychological inquiry, may perhaps, if they should come to the conclusion that they have gained a new idea, be willing to accept along with it a compendious term, having a score of analogies in the language, to afford it definite expression.

Finally, if the sketch I have attempted to draw of the evolution of the social sentiment appear to possess historical truth, it remains only to remark, that the long progress upward of mankind, which I have traced from the primeval reign of violence and antagonism to that of sympathy and mutual help, has not supplied us with the slightest clew to the mystery of how, at each successive stage, and as the higher sentiment dawns, there is a corresponding overruling inward command to *follow* the higher, and disregard the lower impulse. Nothing in the progress of the *emotion* explains either the existence or progress of the moral sense of *obligation*, any more than the anatomy of a horse explains how he is found with bit and bridle. Other things grow, nay, every thing in our nature grows, as well as these emotions. Every taste alters, every sentiment develops; but nothing within us corresponding to the moral sense develops simultaneously alongside of them, setting the seal of approval on the tastes and feelings of adult life, and of disapprobation on those of childhood. If, then, this regulative principle, or intuition of a duty to follow the higher emotion, and renounce the lower, stand out no less inexplicable when we have traced the long history of one of the chief emotions *to be regulated*, we have surely obtained at least a negative reply to the desolating doctrine recently introduced,—that the moral sense in man is only the social instinct of the brute modified under the conditions of human existence. These cultivated instincts, rising into humane emotions, are not the moral sense *itself*, but only that which the moral sense *works upon;* not that which, in any way, explains the ethical choice of good, and rejection of evil, but merely the good and evil things regarding which the choice is exercised. *Whence* we derive the solemn sense of duty to give place to the higher emotion, rather than to the lower (a sense which, undoubtedly, grows simultaneously with the growth of the emotions which it controls), is another problem whose solution cannot here be attempted. One remark only need be made to forestall a commonplace of the new phase of utilitarianism. We are told that our personal intuitions of duty are the inherited prejudices of our ancestors in favor of the kind of actions which have proved, on experience, to be most conducive to the general welfare of the community; or, as Mr. Martineau well calls them, "the capitalized experiences of utility and social coercion, the record of ancestral fears and satisfactions stored in the brain, and re-appearing with divine pretensions only because their animal origin is forgotten." If this be the case, how does it happen that we have all acquired, in these days, a very clear intuition that it is our duty to preserve the lives of the aged, of sufferers by disease, and of deformed children? The howl of indignation which followed the publication of a humanely intended scheme of euthanasia for shortening the existence of such persons for their *own* benefit, may afford us a measure of what the feelings of modern Christendom would be, were some new Lycurgus to propose to extinguish them for the good of the commonwealth. Yet what, in truth, is this ever-growing sense of the infinite sacredness of human life, but a sentiment tending directly to counteract the interest of the community at large? Mr. Greg has clearly expounded, that our compassion for the feeble and the sickly defeats, as regards the human race, the beneficent natural law of the "Survival of the Fittest;"[1] and Mr. Galton considers it to involve nothing short of a menace to the civilization whence it has sprung. Nature kills off such superfluous lives among the brutes; and

[1] See the whole remarkable chapter, Enigmas, iii.

savages and Chinese follow Nature, to their great advantage and convenience. Yet even the Chinese do not profess to have any sense of moral obligation to drown their superfluous babies; and we, who ruthlessly entail on our nation all the evils resulting from allowing diseased and deformed people to live and multiply, have actually a "set of the brain" in favor of our own practice, and decidedly against that of the natives of the Flowery Land! Till this enigma be satisfactorily explained, I think we are justified in assuming, that, whencesoever the awful and divine idea of moral duty may have descended to us, it has, at all events, *not* been derived from the inherited prejudices of our ancestors in favor of the kind of actions which are "most conducive to the general welfare of the community," and have even been recognized so to be for thousands of years.

THE LIFE AFTER DEATH.

THE LIFE AFTER DEATH.

I.

EARTHLY minds, no less than heavenly bodies, seem constrained to pursue their walk by a compromise between opposing forces. Our orbits lie halfway between the tracks which we should follow, did we obey exclusively centripetal selfishness or centrifugal love, — the gravitation of the senses, or the upward attractions of the soul. Especially is this compromise observable in the case of our anticipation of prolonged existence after death. Not one man in a thousand lives either as if he relied on these hopes, or renounced them; as if he expected immortality, or resigned himself to annihilation. The average human being never gives entire loose to his passions on the principle, "Let us eat and drink, for to-morrow we die;" but he constantly attaches to the transient concerns of earth an importance, which, if death be a prelude to a nobler existence, is not merely disproportionate, but absurd. The sentiments he entertains towards God are not such as might befit an insect towards him who is preparing to crush it; but neither are they those of a son to a Father, into whose home on high he is assured, ere long, of a welcome. He mourns his departed friends not altogether with despair, but with very little of the confident "hope of a joyful resurrection," which his clergyman officially expresses while he commits their bodies to the ground. He awaits his own demise with regret or resignation, nearly always measured by his happiness or misery in the world he quits, rather than by his expectations of one or the other in that which he is about to enter; but he rarely contemplates the possibility of final loss of consciousness, or fails to project himself eagerly into interests with which, in such contingency, he can have no concern whatever. In a word, he lives and dies so as to secure for himself pretty nearly the maximum of care and sorrow, and the minimum of peace and hope.

It is in a certain degree inevitable, that some such indecision should pertain to our feelings regarding the life after death. Our belief that such a life awaits us is derived (as I hope presently to show), not from any definite demonstration, such as is furnished to us by the logical understanding, but from the testimony of our moral and spiritual faculties, which varies in force with the more or less perfect working condition of those faculties at all times. Yet there can be few thoughtful men or women amongst us who do not desire some more equable tenure of the priceless "hope full of immortality." If, during the years of multifold youthful enthusiasms, or of world-engrossed middle age, the threat of death seemed dreamlike (so full was our life), and the further hope beyond a dream within a dream, too faint and filmy for thought to seize upon it, such capacity for indifference inevitably passes away with the shock of a bereavement, an illness, or the symptoms of failing strength; and we marvel how it has been possible for us to forget that interests so near and so stupendous yet hang for us all undetermined in the balance. Or if, in the vivid ecstasy of early religion, it happened to us to think that the joy of once beholding the face of God was enough, and that we were content to die forever the next hour, even this experience, after a time, makes annihilation seem doubly impossible, and prompts the question, which has but one answer, —

"*Can* a finite thing, created in the bounds of time and space,
Can it live, and grow, and love Thee, catch the glory of thy face,
Fade, and die, be gone forever, know no being, have no place?"[1]

And, as the wrong and injustice of the world by degrees force themselves on our awakening consciousness, we learn to appeal with confidence to God, if not on our own behalf, yet for all the miserable and the vice-abandoned, that he should open to them the door of a happier and holier world than they have known below.

And, for mankind at large, the solution of the problem of immortality which will be generally received in the future reconstruction of opinion must prove of incalculable importance. Should the belief in a life after death still remain an article of popular faith after the fall of supernaturalism, then (freed, as it must be, of its dead-weight of the dread of hell) the religion of succeeding generations will possess more than all the influence of the creeds of old; for it will meet human nature on all its noblest sides at once, and insult it on none. On the other hand, if the present well-nigh exclusive devotion to physico-scientific thought end in throwing

[1] Verses, by E. B. Henry King and Co., London.

the spiritual faculties of our nature so far into disuse and discredit as to leave the faith in immortality permanently under a cloud,[1] then it is inevitable that religion will lose half the power it has wielded over human hearts. The God with whom our relations are so insignificant that he has condemned them to terminate at the end of a few short years, — the God whose world contains so many cruel wrongs destined to remain unrectified forever, — the God who cares so little for man's devotion that He *will* "suffer his Holy One to see corruption," — that God may receive our distant homage as the Arbiter of the universe; but it is quite impossible that he should obtain our love. Nor will the results of the general retention, or loss, of the faith in a future life on the morals of mankind, be less significant than those affecting their religion. They will not, I believe, be of the kind vulgarly apprehended. The fear of hell has been vastly overestimated as an engine of police; for the natures which are capable of receiving a practical check to strong passion from anticipations only to be realized in a distant world, are (by the hypothesis) constituted with singularly blended elements of imagination

[1] See the remarks on this subject in Christ in Modern Life, by the Rev. Stopford Brooke, p. 194.

and prudence, the furthest possible from the criminal temperament. And the hope of heaven has been, probably, even less valuable as a moral agent, having spoiled the pure disinterestedness of virtue for thousands, by degrading duty into that "other-worldliness," which is only harder and more selfish than worldliness pure and simple. But, though the loss of the bribes and threats of the life to come would tend little to lower the standard of human virtue, it would be quite otherwise as regards the final closing of all outlook beyond this world, and the shutting-up of morality within the narrow sphere of mortal life. We need an infinite horizon to enable us to form any conception of the grandeur and sanctity of moral distinctions; nor is it possible we should continue to attach to virtue and vice the same profound significance, could we believe their scope to reach no further than our brief span. Theoretically, right and wrong would come to be regarded as of comparatively small importance. Practically, the virtue which must shortly come to an end forever would seem, to the tempted soul, scarcely deserving of effort; and the vice which must lie down harmless in the sinner's grave, too mere a trifle to waste on it remorse or indignation. Life, in short, after we had passed its meridian, would become in our eyes more and more like an autumn garden, wherein it would be vain to plant seeds of good which could never bloom before the frosts of death, and useless to eradicate weeds which must needs be killed ere long, without our labor. Needless to say, that, of that dismal spot, it might surely soon be said, —

> "Between the time of the wind and the snow
> All loathsome things began to grow;"

and that, when winter came at last, none would regret the white shroud it threw over corruption and decay.

Nor ought we to hide from ourselves, that, under such loss of hope in immortality, the highest forms of human heroism must needs disappear, and cease to glorify the world. The old martyrs of the stake and the rack, and modern martyrs of many a wreck and battle-field and hospital, have not braved torture and death *for the sake* of the rewards of paradise; but they have at least believed that their supreme act of virtue and piety did not involve the renunciation, on their part, of all further moral progress, and of all communion with God throughout eternity. It is not easy to see how any virtue is to help a man to renounce virtue, nor even how the love of God is to make him ready to renounce the joy of his love forever. Deprived, then, of its boundless scope, human morality must necessarily be dwarfed more and more in each successive generation, till, in comparison of the mere animal life (which would inevitably come to the front), the nobler part in us would dwindle to a vanishing-point, and the man return to the ape.

What are the probabilities that the faith in immortality may escape the wreck of the supernatural creeds, and what are the spars and rafts, if any such there be, to which individually we may most safely cling? To answer these questions, it is necessary to cast a glance around us on the present attitude of thinking men on the matter. A few books and articles — among which I would specially direct the reader's attention to four of Mr. Stopford Brooke's admirable discourses — give some hint of the currents of thought now passing over us;[1] but there is little doubt, that, before long, a much larger share of attention will be given to the subject, and that it will form in truth the battle-ground for one of the most decisive struggles

[1] A miserable pseudo-scientific treatise, *Le Lendemain de la Mort*, by Louis Figuier, has already run through four or five editions in as many months. Simple readers ask for bread, and the Frenchman drops into their mouths a bonbon.

in the history of the mental progress of our race. Our standpoint at this moment is somewhat peculiar. We are losing the old ground, and have not yet found footing on the new.

The delusion which has prevailed so long in England, that we acquire such truths as the existence of God and our own immortality by means of logical demonstration, appears to be slowly passing away. We hardly imagine now, as English divines from Paley to Whately habitually took for granted, that, if we convince (or "vanquish") a man in argument concerning them, his next step must infallibly be to embrace them heartily, as the Arabs did Islam, at the point of the sword. Especially we begin to perceive that we have been on the wrong track in dealing with the belief in a future life; nay, that we have been twice misled in the matter. The old popular creed having presented the doctrine to us as a matter of historical revelation, we were first trained to think of it as a fact guaranteed by a book, and, accordingly, of course to be ascertained by the criticism of that book. Our eternal life was secure, if we could demonstrate the authenticity and canonicity of certain Greek manuscripts; but, were the Bible to prove untrustworthy, our only valid ground of hope would be lost, and the immortality (which, in the face of Egypt and India, we were complacently assured had been only "brought to light through the gospel") would be re-consigned to the blackness of darkness. From this primary mistake, those who think freely in our day are pretty nearly emancipated. The "apocalpytic side of Christianity" has ceased to satisfy even those religious liberals who still take its moral and spiritual part as absolutely divine; and the halting logic which argued from the supposed corporeal resurrection of the Second Person of the Trinity to the spiritual survival of the mass of mankind, has been so often exposed, that it can scarcely again be produced in serious controversy.[1]

[1] That the death of Christ, not his supposed resurrection, furnishes a strong argument in favor of immortality, will be shown by and by. Is it not probable that the great myth of his bodily revival owes its origin simply to the overwhelming impression which the scene of the Passion must have made on the disciples, transforming their hitherto passive Pharisaic or Essene belief in a future life into the vivid personal faith that *such a soul could not have become extinct?* In a lesser way, the grave of a beloved friend has been to many a man the birthplace of his faith; and it is obvious, that, in the case of Christ, every condition was fulfilled which would raise such sudden conviction to the height of passionate fervor. The first words of the disciples to one another on that Easter morn may well have been, "He is not dead. His spirit is this day in paradise, among the sons of God." It was the simplest consequence of their veneration for him, that they

While we have escaped, however, from the error of supernaturalism, a second, and no less fatal mistake has risen in our way. The prevalent passion of the age for physical science has brought the relation of physiology to the problem of a future life altogether into the foreground of our attention, as if it formed the only important consideration; and of course on this side there was never any hope of a successful solution. Apologists of vivisectors made it, indeed, their excuse that those modern sworn tormentors were "seeking the religion of the future" in the brains of tortured dogs; but no one, I presume, ever seriously expected any other result than that which we behold. No

should feel such assurance, and give it utterance with prophetic fire. In that age of belief in miracles, this new-born faith in the immortality of a righteous soul was inevitably clothed almost immediately in materialistic shape; and, by the time the Gospels were written, it had become stereotyped in traditions which we can class only as Jewish ghost-stories.

If this conjecture be admitted, we are absolved equally from the acceptance, as historical, of the monster miracle of the New Testament, and from the insufferable alternative of recourse to some hypothesis of fraud, collusion, or mistake. It cannot have been on any such base or haphazard incident that the reliance of Christendom has rested for eighteen centuries. Even with its blended note of human error, it is, after all, the reverberation of that earthquake which rent the hearts of those who watched on Calvary, and tore the veil of mortality from their eyes, which has ever since echoed down the ages, and still sounds in our ears.

ossiculum luz, no "infrangible bone," such as the rabbins averred was the germ of the resurrection-body, no "indestructible monad," such as Leibnitz dreamed, has come to light, and no "gray matter," or "hippocampus," or multiplied convolutions of the human brain, are found to afford the faintest suggestion of a life beyond mortality. The only verdict which can be wrung from Science is, that the cessation of all conscious being at death is "not proven." She recognizes a mysterious somewhat termed "Life," whose nature she has yet failed to ascertain, and concerning whose possible changes she is therefore silent. And, further, having proved that no force is ever destroyed, she admits that it is open to conjecture, that the force of the human will may have its "conservation" in some mode whereby conscious agency may indefinitely be prolonged. But, beyond this point, Science refuses to say one word to encourage the hope of immortality. She remains neutral, even when she forbears to utter oracles of despair. Nay, rather is she no prophetess at all, but may better be likened to some gaunt sign-post beside the highway of life, pointing with one wooden arm to the desolate waste, and with the other to fair fields and fresh pastures, but giving no response to our cry of anguish, "Whither have our beloved ones gone?"

Nor will the analogies of Nature help us better than the physiological analysis of our own frames. The "fifty"—nay, rather the five thousand—seeds, of which "she scarcely brings but one to bear," and the wrecks of the myriad forms of animal life which lie embedded in the rocks under our feet, reveal the lavishness of her waste. All the sweet old similes in which our forefathers found comfort—the reviving grain, "sown in corruption, and raised in power;" the crawling larva endued with wings as Psyche's butterfly—fail, when seriously criticised, to afford any parallel with the hoped-for resurrection of the human soul. Nay, Nature seems constantly to mock us by reviving in preference her humblest products, and bringing up, year after year, to the sunshine of spring, the clover and the crocus and the daisy, while manly strength and womanly beauty lie perishing beneath the flowers, hid forever in the hopeless ruin of the grave.

And, lastly, there are certain arguments which may be classed as metaphysical, which were once generally relied on as affording demonstration of a future life. The value of these arguments, from Plato's downwards,—that the idea of a dead soul is absurd; that the soul, being "simple" and "one," cannot be "dissolved;" that, being "immaterial," it cannot die, &c., — is extremely difficult to estimate. It is possible they may point to great truths; but it is manifest that they all hinge on certain assumptions concerning the nature of the soul, and the supposed antithesis between mind and matter, which we are learning each day to regard with more distrust; in fact, to treat as insoluble problems. In this direction also, then, it is not too much to conclude we cannot hope to find a satisfactory answer to our inquiry.

When we have dismissed the expectation of obtaining the desired solution, either from a supernatural revelation, or from physics or metaphysics, where do we stand? We are left to face, on one hand, a number of very heavy presumptions against the survival of consciousness after death, and, on the other hand, the sole class of considerations which remain to be opposed to them.

The presumptions against survival are so plain and numerous, that none of us can fail to be impressed with their force. There is, first, the obvious fact that every thing we have seen of a man perishes, to our certain knowledge, in his grave, and passes into other organic and inorganic forms. The assumption is physiologically baseless that something, and that something his conscious self, lives elsewhere. And, starting from this baseless assumption, we find no foothold for even a conjecture of *how* he is transferred to his new abode, *where* in the astronomical universe that abode can be, and *what* can be the conditions of existence and consciousness, without a brain, or a single one of our organs of the senses. The fact that injuries to the brain in this life are capable of clouding a man's mind, and distorting his will in frenzy or idiotcy, presses severely against the assumption, that the entire dissolution of that brain will leave intellect and volition perfect and free. Nor do even these enormous difficulties exhaust the obstacles in the way. If man be immortal, he must have become an immortal being at some point in his development after the first beginning of physical life. But to name even a plausible date for so stupendous a change in his destiny is utterly impossible ; and the new theory of evolution saddles us yet with another analogous difficulty, namely, to designate the links in the chain of generations between the ascidian and the sage, when the mortal creature gave birth to an heir of immortality. It is almost impossible to overstate the weight of these and other presumptions of a similar kind against the belief in a life after death. Let it be granted that they are as heavy as they could be without absolutely disproving the point in question, and making the belief logically absurd. They render, at all events, the fact of immortality so *improbable*, that to restore the balance, and make it probable, an immense equiponderant consideration becomes indispensable.

Where is that counterweight to be found? What can we cast into the scale which shall outweigh these presumptions? Certainly nothing in the way of direct answers to them, nor of plausible hypotheses to explain how the conditions of future being may possibly be carried on. Confronted by the challenge to produce such hypotheses, we can but say, with one of the greatest men of science of the age, that, "the further we advance in the path of science, the more the infinite possibilities of Nature are revealed to us;" and, among those possibilities, there must needs be the possibility of another life for man. Beyond this, we cannot proffer a word; and it must be some consideration altogether of another character which can afford any thing like a positive reason for believing in immortality in opposition to the terrible array of presumptions on the other side. That consideration, so sorely needed, is, I believe, to be found, nay, is found already by the great mass of mankind, in FAITH, —faith in its true sense of TRUST in goodness and justice and fidelity and love, and in all these things impersonated in the Lord of life and death. Not the supernatural argument, nor yet the physical, nor the metaphysical, but the *moral*, is the real counterpoise to all the difficulties in the way of belief in a life beyond the grave.

That this is the true ground of whatever confidence we can rationally entertain on the subject, is, I think, clear on very short reflection. It has been but partially recognized, indeed, that such is the case; and the teachers who have undertaken to demonstrate immortality on natural grounds have very commonly presented their moral arguments as if they were purely inductive, and belonged to the same class of logical proofs as we have sought for in vain in physics and metaphysics. But their syllogisms, when carefully examined, will invariably be found to involve a major term, which is not a fact of knowledge, but only a dogma of faith. They conduct us halfway across the gulf by means of stepping-stones of facts and inductions, and then invite us to complete our transit by swimming. They open our cause in the court of the intellect, and then move it for decision to the equity-chamber of the heart. A few pages hence, I shall hope to give this assertion full illustration. For the present, it will be sufficient to remind the reader that the arguments usually drawn from the general consciousness of mankind, from the many injustices of the world, from the incompleteness of moral progress in this life, &c., all involve, at the crucial poïnt, the assumption that we possess some guaranty that mankind will *not* be deceived, that justice *will* triumph eventually, and that human progress is the concern of a Power whose purposes cannot fail. Were the faith which supplies such warrants to prove irresponsive to the call, the whole elaborate argument which preceded the appeal would be seen at once to fall to the ground. If, then, the strength of a chain must be measured by that of its most fragile link, it is clear that the value in sum total of all such arguments, however multiplied or ingeniously stated, is neither more nor less than that which we may be disposed to assign to simple faith. It is a value precisely tantamount to that of our moral and religious intuitions, — to the value (as I hope presently to show) of *all* such intuitions culminating in one point together. But, beyond this, it is nothing.

This conclusion, however distasteful it may be to us, is one which eminently harmonizes with all we can learn respecting the method of the divine tuition of souls. There is one kind of knowledge which the Creator has appointed shall be acquired by the busy intellect, and which, when so acquired, is held in inalienable possession. There is another kind of knowledge which he gives to faithful and obedient hearts, and which even the truest of them hold on the precarious tenure of sustained faith and unrelaxing obedience. The future world assuredly belongs to this latter class of knowledge. It is, as one of the greatest of living teachers has said, "a part of our religion, not a branch of our geography." Why it is so, and why our passionate longings for more sense-satisfying information cannot be indulged, we can even partially see; for we may perceive that it would instantaneously destroy the perspective of this life, and nullify the whole present system of moral tuition by earthly joys and chastisements. The mental chaos into which those persons obviously fall who in our day imagine that they have obtained tangible, audible, and visible proofs of another life, supplies evidence of the ruinous results which would follow, were any such corporeal access to the other world actually opened to mankind.

Let us, then, courageously face the conclusion which we seem to have reached. The key which must open the door of hope beyond the grave will never be found by fumbling among the heterogeneous stores of the logical understanding. Like the one with which the Pilgrim unlocked the dungeon of Giant Despair's Castle, it is hidden in our own breasts, — given to us long ago by the Lord of the Way.

This essay is not the place, even were I possessed of the needful ability, to determine the true "Grammar of Assent" as regards such faith as is now in question. I must limit myself to addressing those readers who are prepared to concede that spiritual things are "spiritually discerned," and moral things morally; and that the human moral sense and religious sentiment are something more than untrustworthy delusions. To those who doubt all this, who believe in food and houses and railways and stocks and gravitation and electricity, but not in self-sacrificing love or justice or God, I can say nothing. The argument has been shown to have no standpoint on any grounds they will admit. That they should disbelieve in immortality is the perfectly logical outcome of their other disbeliefs. It would be entirely inconsequent and irrational for them to believe in it.

Assuming, then, that I address men and women who believe in God and justice and love, I proceed to endeavor to show how, even should they stand appalled by the difficulties of belief in immortality, they may yet oppose to those difficulties moral arguments so numerous and irrefragable, that the scale may well turn on the side of belief. I hope to show, that, by many different but converging lines, Faith uniformly points to a life after death, and that, if we follow her guidance in any one direction implicitly, we are invariably led to the same conclusion. Nay, more: I think it may be demonstrated that we cannot stop short of this culmination, and afterwards retain intact our faith in any thing beyond matters of sense and experience. Every idea we can form of justice, love, duty, is truncated and imperfect, if we deny them the extension of eternity; and, as for our conception of God, I see not how any one who has realized the "riddle of the painful earth" can thenceforth call him "good," unless he believe that the solution is yet to be given to that dark problem hereafter.

The following are some of the channels in which faith flows towards immortality.

I. There is one unendurable thought: it is, that justice may fail to be done in time or in eternity. This thought makes the human soul writhe like a trampled worm. Other ideas are sad, even agonizing; but this one cannot be borne. No courage, no virtue, no unselfishness, will help us to bear it. The better we are, the more insufferable it is. To receive it into the soul is madness. On the other hand, every threat besides, however sorrowful or terrible, if it be but overshadowed by the sense "it will be just," becomes endurable, nay, is followed by a sort of awful calm. Could we even feel certain that our guilt merited eternal perdition, then the doom of hell would bring to us only dumb despair. Something greater than ourselves within us would say to the wailings of our self-pity, "Peace, be still." But let us only doubt that there is any justice here or hereafter; let us think that wrong and tyranny may be finally triumphant, and goodness and heroism ultimately defeated, punished, and derided; and, lo! there surges up from the very depths of our souls a high and stern remonstrance, an appeal which should make the hollow heavens resound with our indignation and our rebellion.

The religions of the world, well nigh in the proportion in which they deserve to be called religions, and not mere dreams of awe and wonder, are the expressions of the universal human aspiration after justice. Even the Buddhist creed (whose acceptance by the myriads of Eastern Asia for two millenniums gives the lie to so many of our theories, and seems to show human nature different under another sky), — even this abnormal creed insists that righteousness rules everywhere and forever, even when it teaches there is no righteous Ruler on high, or, "peradventure, he sleepeth" in the eternal slumber of Nirvana. The doctrine of Karma — that every good and every evil action inexorably brings forth fruit of reward or fruit of punishment, in this life or some other life to come — is the confession of three hundred million souls, that, if they can endure to live without God, they yet cannot live without justice. Nay, it is more. It is evidence that human reason can accept such a blank absurdity as the idea that the unintelligent elements may bring about moral order sooner than the human spirit can rest satisfied that such moral order is nowhere to be found. Gravitation and electricity may weigh self-sacrifice and purity in their balances, and the winds and waves may measure out the punishment of cruelty and falsehood; but virtue cannot be without reward, nor can the crimes which human tribunals fail to reach escape retribution forever.

The shapes which this desire of justice assumes in the earlier stages of human thought are, of course, rude and materialistic in the extreme. Men cannot expect from Nemesis, or Karma, or Jehovah, higher justice than they have begun to apprehend as the law of their own dealings. But everywhere throughout mythology, history, and poetry, we may trace the parallel lines of the moral growth of each nation, and the corresponding development of its belief, that, over and above human justice, there is a justice-working Power, personal or impersonal, controlling all events, and making war and plague and famine, the earthquake and the storm, the punishments of crime, and health and victory, length of days, abundant wealth and numerous progeny, the rewards of virtue.

The obvious failure of the exhibition of any such overruling justice in multitudes of instances has commonly driven the bewildered observers to devise explanations, more or less ingenious, of each particular case, but rarely, if ever, to the much more logical course of abandoning the expectation of such justice. Half the myths of the elder nations are nothing more than hypotheses invented to justify Providence, and explain consistently with equity some striking inequality in the distribution of prosperity and adversity. As negroes and Canaanites underwent more cruel oppressions than other races, their supposed progenitor, Ham, must have incurred some special curse. As women endure peculiar sufferings, and are in early times altogether enslaved by men, so Eve must have merited the punishment of bringing forth children in sorrow, and being " ruled over " by her husband. As the cities of the plain were overwhelmed by a terrific convulsion, so it was certain Sodom and Gomorrah were more wicked than Memphis or Thebes. In Grecian fable, the calamities which befell the house of Œdipus presupposed

> " The ill-advised transgression of old Laius;"

and even such trivial matters as the blackness of the crow and the chatter of the magpie might be traced to the punishment of a human offender transformed into the bird, whose whole race thenceforward, like that of Adam, was destined to bear the penalty of " original sin."

Nor do the monuments of the graver thoughts of mankind bear less emphatic testimony than mythology to the universal desire to "see justice done." Beginning with the Vedas and Genesis, Homer and Herodotus, we may trace the straining effort of every writer to "point a moral" of reward and punishment, even when the facts to be dealt with lent but faint color to the lesson that perfidious chiefs will always be defeated, and good kings crowned with victory and prosperity. The story of ruined cities is always told in the same spirit: —

> "They rose while all the depths of guilt their vain creators sounded;
> They fell because on fraud and force their corner-stones were founded."

In every age and nation, epics, dramas, and popular legends, wherever they may be found, either directly aim to represent what we have significantly learned to name "poetic justice," or pay the idea still deeper homage by founding the tragedy of the piece on the failure of justice. Never is the notion absent, either from the ethical poets, such as the author of Job, Euripides, Dante, or Milton, or from those who have followed the principle of art for art's sake, — Æschylus, Shakspeare, and Goethe. Each of us in the course of life exemplifies the cycle of human thought in the matter. In childhood we read history with impatient longing for the triumph of patriots and heroes, and the overthrow of their oppressors; and we prefer ancient history to modern, because it seems to offer a clearer field for the vindication of ethical ideas. In youth we find delight in the romances which exhibit virtue as crowned with success, and wickedness defeated; and it is invariably with a mingled sense of surprise and indignation, that we fling down the first tale which leaves us at its conclusion with our legitimate anticipations of such a *dénoûment* unsatisfied. To this hour the play-going public, which represents the youthful-mindedness of the community, refuses to sanction any picture of life wherein, ere the curtain falls, the hero is not vindicated from all aspersion, and the villain punished and exposed. Only far on in life, and in literary culture, do we begin, with many misgivings, mournfully to recognize the superior verisimilitude of tales which depict virtue as receiving no reward, and guilt no punishment, in this world.

The question, "How mankind has come to possess this confidence in Nemesis?" will, of course, be answered differently according to our various theories of the origin of all moral sentiments. Dr. Johnson ascribes our passion for justice to the simple source of fear lest we should personally suffer from injustice, — an hypothesis which would be highly satisfactory, provided, in the first place, we were all so good that we had every thing to hope and nothing to dread from justice; and, secondly, provided our interest in justice never extended backward in time, and far off into distance, immeasurably beyond the circle of events in which we can ever have personal concern. The theory which would accord with the general neo-utilitarian doctrine now in fashion would be a little more philosophic than this. Our modern teachers would probably tell us, that our expectation of justice is the result of the "set" of the human brain, fixed by experience through countless generations. As our sense of duty is, on their showing, derived from the repeated observation of the utility of virtuous actions, so, on the same principle, our expectation of justice must come from numberless observations of instances wherein justice has been illustriously manifested. It is, indeed, easier to see how the constant association of the ideas of guilt and punishment, virtue and reward, formed by such observations, should produce the expectation to see one always follow the other, than it is to understand how the observation of the utility of virtue should impress upon us the solemn categoric imperative,

"Be virtuous." The expectation of justice might be merely an intellectual presumption of the same character as our anticipation of the recurrence of day and night, or any other phenomena associated in unbroken sequence. The sense of duty is a practical spur to action, whose relation to its supposed origin of long-observed utility remains, when all is said, a "mystic extension" of that prosaic idea altogether unaccountable.

But there is, unfortunately, a difficulty in the way of availing ourselves of this easy solution of the origin of the universal expectation of justice. It is hard to see how the "set of our brains" towards such expectation could have been formed by experience, considering that no generation seems to have been favored by any such experience at all. To produce such a "set," it would (by the hypothesis) be necessary that the instances wherein justice was plainly exhibited should be so common as to constitute the rule, and those wherein it failed exceptions too rare to hinder the solid mass of conviction from settling in the given direction. Like a sand-bar formed by the action of the tides and currents, our "set of brain" can only come from uniform impressions; and, were the angle of pressure to shift continually, it is clear it could take no permanent shape whatever. Now, does any one imagine that such uniform and perspicuous vindication of justice in the course of events has been witnessed by mankind at any age of the world's history? Is there any thing like it impressed upon our own minds as we read, day after day, of public affairs, or reflect on the occurrences of private life? Are we accustomed to see well-meant actions always followed by reward, and evil ones infallibly productive of failure or disgrace? Even at the present stage of moral advance in public opinion and in righteous legislation, can we flatter ourselves that things are so arranged as to secure the unvarying triumph of probity, veracity, modesty, and all the other virtues, and the exemplary overthrow of fraud, impudence, and selfishness? Suppose a cynic to hold the opposite thesis, and maintain that we are continually punished for our generosity and simplicity, and rewarded for cunning and hypocrisy. Should we be able to overwhelm him with a mass of instances to the contrary, ready at a moment's notice in our memory? Can we imagine (as a single illustration of the subject) that the thousands of adulterating tradesmen and fraudulent merchants in England at this moment would pursue their evil courses so consistently, did daily experience really warn those sagacious persons that "honesty is the best policy"? Of course, as we recede towards times when laws were far less just than they are now, and oppression and violence were far more common, the scene becomes darker and less hopeful. Looking back through the vista of the historic and prehistoric ages, the probability of finding a reign of Astræa, when right always triumphed over might, becomes necessarily "fine by degrees, and beautifully less," till we are driven to the conclusion, that, if we owe the set of our brains towards justice to the experience of our ancestors, that "set" must have been given when justice was rarely manifest at all, "and the earth was full of violence and cruel habitations." The share which the purely physical laws have had in punishing moral offences has, doubtless, been always what it is now; and that share, to all our knowledge, is extremely obscure. If health and longevity are the frequent accompaniment of one class of virtues, disease and death are equally often incurred by another; nor is there any sort of token that abundant harvests or blighted fields, prosperous voyages or tempest-driven wrecks, have any relation to the moral character of the mariner or the agriculturist, or that, from the observation of such events for sixty centuries, a theory of morals could possibly have been evolved. Practically, it is obvious that men do not see wickedness, and infer punishment, but, rather, when they see punishment, they infer wickedness. A thousand tyrants had been more cruel than Herod, and yet had never been "smitten by God" with the portentous disease of which the Idumæan died. A hundred invaders before Xerxes had trampled on the necks of conquered nations, but no Nemesis had deserved a temple for rebuking their pride, no Hellespontine waves had risen in tempest to destroy their fleets.

It is not experience, then, it never could be experience gained in such a world as ours, which has impressed on the brain of man its "set" towards the expectation of justice, or inspired its string of accordant aphorisms, that "the wicked will come to a fearful end," that "murder will out," that "honesty is the best policy," and that "the righteous" man is never forsaken, nor his seed destined to "beg their bread." From some other source, remote from experience, we must have derived an impression which we persistently maintain, and endeavor to verify in defiance of ever-recurring failure and disappointment. What that source may be, it does not vitally concern the present argument to determine. Probably the expectation may most safely be treated as the imperfect intellectual expression of a great moral intuition, forming an ultimate fact of our moral constitution. All such deep but dim intuitions, when rendered into definite ideas, are necessarily imperfect, and liable to error. We err both as to the time and the form in which they are to be fulfilled. We feel that justice ought to be supreme; but, when we translate that sentiment into an idea, we fondly picture the great scheme of the universe developed within the sphere of our vision. Like children possessed of a magnet, we imagine the pole to which it points may be found in the neighboring field. Our magnet is true enough; but

> "The far-off Divine Event,
> Towards which the whole creation moves,"

is beyond our horizon. And, similarly, we give to our spiritual intuitions materialistic forms, which are far from rendering them veraciously. The concrete, the visible, the tangible, are inevitably the earliest expressions even of our highest sentiments. We feel the majesty of God, and picture him seated on a throne. We feel his justice; and the myth of a day of judgment rises before us. In like manner, our intuitive expectation that virtue will be rewarded clothes itself in all manner of carnal shapes of crowns and riches; and our expectation that vice will be punished, in similar shapes of pain and infamy. At a further stage of human thought, when the anticipation of physical reward and punishment in this life has been, of necessity, postponed to, or supplemented by, those of another world, we substitute the almost equally materialistic rewards of Elysium and Paradise, or penalties of Jehanum and Hell. It needs a long course of progress to get beyond such ideas, and learn to render spiritual sentiments spiritually, and moral ones morally only. It militates nothing against the veracity of the original profound intuition of justice, that hitherto men have thus mistranslated it into the promise of a speedy settlement of the great account in the gross earthly coin of physical good or evil here or hereafter. That intuition will, doubtless, be far more perfectly fulfilled in the grander scope of eternity, and by means of the transcendent joys and sorrows of the spiritual life. When we have advanced far enough to feel that all other good and evil are as nothing in comparison of these, it will be easy to see how the Supreme Justice may use those tremendous instruments in its ultimate dealings with merit and demerit, and reward virtue, not with the dross of earthly health or wealth, or of celestial crowns and harps, but with the only boon the true saint desires, — even the sense of union with God; and punish vice, not with disease and disgrace, nor with the fire and worms of hell, but with the most awful of all penalties, — the severance of the soul from divine light and love. No one who has obtained even a glimmering of the meaning of these spiritual realities can hesitate to confess that his soul's most passionate craving after justice may be superabundantly fulfilled in such ways, even in worlds not necessarily divided into distinct realms of reward and punishment, but where, as in another school, and higher stage of being, our spiritual part shall have freer scope, and leave the carnal in the shade.

We now proceed to the next step of the argument, which, as yet, makes no appeal beyond experience. We assume that mankind at large anticipates and desires that justice may be done. *Is* it done in this world? We have seen that it is not outwardly or perspicuously vindicated: is there, nevertheless, room left to suppose that it possibly may have been fulfilled in ways hidden from us, such as the satisfaction of a *mens conscia recti*, or the misery of secret remorse?

The answer to this question has been commonly evaded, or the question itself blinked, under what I conceive to be a most mistaken sense of reverence to God. Sometimes we are told it is not for us to say what is justice; and sometimes we are reminded how little we can guess the hidden joys and pangs of our fellow-creatures, and how easily these may counterbalance all external conditions. I do not think the case is so obscure as is alleged; and I am quite sure that reverence for God never requires us to close our eyes to facts. What is in question is not any abstract or *occulta justitia*, but precisely *our idea of* justice, — that expectation, which, by some means or other, has been raised in the hearts of men from the beginning of history till now. Is *that* fulfilled, or room left for its fulfilment, in this world? I do not hesitate to affirm that it is not fulfilled, and that, in thousands of cases, there is no room left wherein it can possibly be fulfilled up to the hour of death. No retribution which could satisfy it has had space to be exhibited. The tyrant, with his last breath, has crowned the pyramid of his crimes, and died with the smile of gratified cruelty on his lips. The martyr has expired in tortures of body and of mind. Nothing that can be imagined to have been experienced of remorse in the one soul, or of joy in the other, would rectify the balance.

Two classes of readers will demur to what I have to say on this topic. One will take the injustice of the world to be so notorious a fact as to need no elaborate proof, and will resent as superfluous any attempt to establish it. The other will be shocked by the naked statement, and may even contradict it with impatience. Let us clear up our position a little. What a well-developed sense of justice requires for its satisfaction is, that no one being shall suffer more than he has deserved, or undergo the penalty of another's guilt. It is nothing to the satisfaction of such justice, that nine hundred and ninety-nine persons are treated with exactest equity, if the humblest and meanest bears sufferings disproportioned to his deserts, nor if the punishment which A has merited falls upon B, and the reward of the virtue of C be enjoyed by D. A single instance of positive injustice done to a single individual would suffice to decide the point. Justice is not fulfilled on earth, if there has been one such case since creation.

Now, will any one dispute that such cases have occurred, not singly, but by hundreds and thousands? Of course there are innumerable instances, seemingly of crying injustice, in which, could we see behind the scenes, and know all the bearings of the matter, we should find no injustice at all. But there are, also, other instances in which, rationally speaking, it is certain there was injustice; and no further knowledge conceivable could alter our judgment. With all reverence, I will endeavor to state one such case, about which there can be little obscurity.

Jesus Christ was assuredly one of the holiest of men. He died in undeserved tortures; and at the supreme hour of his agony he cried out in despair, "My God, why hast thou forsaken me?" Instead of flooding his departing soul with the rapturous vision which might have neutralized all the horrors of the cross, it pleased the Father, whom he loved as no man had loved him before, to withdraw all consciousness of his presence, and to leave him to expire in darkness and doubt. That ancient story, stripped of all its misleading supernaturalism, seems to me the sufficient evidence that God reserves his justice for eternity.

It is not only the crimes and merits of the death-hour to which justice fails to mete due measure upon earth. Nothing is more obvious than that men are continually doomed to suffer for the evil-doing of others, and that the good which one has sown another reaps. Health and disease, honor and ignominy, wealth and poverty, every thing we can name in the way of external good and evil, come to us more often by the virtue and vice of our parents and neighbors than by any merit or demerit of our own.

Again: the enormous inequality in the distribution of penalties for similar offences leaves a huge mass of injustice which it is impossible to suppose is often providentially rectified in this life. For myself, I do not hesitate to say that the intolerable cruelty with which sins of unchastity in women are visited all over the world, in comparison of the immunity from disgrace enjoyed by profligate men, decides for me the question. Could we realize the reflections of many a poor wretch banished from her home for her first transgression, and driven on helplessly, scourged by hunger and infamy, deeper and deeper into ruin, till she lies wrecked in body and soul, — could we understand her feelings as she compares her lot with that of the man who first tempted her to sin, and whose fault has never stood in the way of his prosperity or reputation, — we should then learn somewhat of how the supposed justice of the world appears from another side from that on which the happy behold it.

In a world where such things happen every day, is it possible to maintain that Providence trims the balance of justice on this side the grave, or that the inner life's history, if revealed to us, would rectify any apparent outward inequality? The horror of such cases lies precisely in this,—that the hideously excessive punishment of the one sinner consists in the fact that she is forced helplessly into the deepest moral pollution; while the light penalty of the other leaves him lifelong space for restoration to self-respect and virtue.

When we go back from our own age of comparative equity to darker times, or pass to the contemplation of the wrongs suffered in semi-barbarous countries, the impressions of injustice multiply and deepen. We think of the hundred thousand helpless creatures burnt to death for the impossible crime of witchcraft; the victims of bigotry or statecraft who have languished out their lives in the dungeons of the Inquisition, of the Bastille, of every castle which frowned over the plains of mediæval Europe; of the myriads who suffered by that huge mockery of justice, the question by torture; of the untold miseries of the slaves and serfs of classic and modern times; and, finally, of the crowning mystery of all, the woful sufferings of innocent little babes and harmless brutes: and as these things pass before us, instead of doubting whether justice sometimes fails, we begin to doubt whether all history be not the record of its failure; and, like Shelley, we are ready to talk of "this *wrong* world."

What does Faith say now? Surely she stakes her whole authority on the assertion that there is another life where such failures of justice will be rectified? The moral argument for immortality, drawn from the consideration of its necessity to give ethical completion to the order of Providence, is quite irrefragable. Either moral arguments have no practical validity, or in this case, at all events, we may rely upon the conclusion to which they point. Man's noblest and most disinterested passion — a passion which may well be deemed the supreme manifestation of the divine element in his nature — will, if death be the end of existence, have proved a miserable delusion; while God himself will prove to have created us, children of the dust, to love and hope for justice, but himself to disregard justice on the scale of a disappointed world.

I have devoted so large a space to this particular line of considerations in favor of a life after death, because I conceive that it has hardly received all the attention it deserves, or been generally stated as broadly as is requisite to exhibit its enormous force. We are not unfrequently reminded that our personal sense of justice is unsatisfied in this world; but it is rarely set forth, that it is the sacred thirst of the whole human race for justice which is defrauded, if there be no world beyond. We are often exhorted to hope that the Lord of conscience will not prove himself less just towards us than he requires us mortals to be to one another; but we are not bidden resolutely and with filial confidence to say — the more boldly, so much the more reverently — either man is immortal, or God is *not just.*

II. Another line of thought leading to the same conclusion lies parallel with the above, but can here be only briefly indicated. Creation, as we behold it, presents a scene in which not only justice fails to be completed, but no single purpose, such as we can attribute for a moment to a good and wise Creator, is thoroughly worked out or fulfilled. If we take the lowest hypothesis, and say he meant us merely to be happy, — to have just such a preponderance of pleasure over pain as should make existence, on the whole a boon, and not a curse, — then it is clear that there are multitudes with regard to whom his purpose fails; as, for example, the poor babes who come into the world diseased, and who die, after weeks or months of pain, without enjoyment of any kind. And if we take a more worthy view of the purpose of creation, and suppose that God has made us, and placed us in this world of trial, to attain the highest end of finite beings, namely, virtue, and union with his own Divine Spirit, then still more obviously, for thousands of men and women, this blessed purpose is abortive; for their mortal life has ended in sin, and utter alienation from God and goodness. If God be wise, he cannot have made his creatures for ends he knew they would never reach; nor, if he be good, can he have made them only for suffering, or only for sin. There is no escape from the conclusion to which faith points unhesitatingly; namely, to a world wherein the beneficent designs of God will finally be carried out.

As the preceding argument appealed to the justice of God, so this one hinges on his goodness and his wisdom. It is essentially a theistic argument, as distinguished from the pantheistic glorification of intellectual greatness. The pantheist says that a philospher *ought* to be immortal; for he is the crown of things. The theist says that a tortured slave, a degraded woman, *must* be immortal; for God's creature could not have been made for torture and pollution. To minds which have been wont to ponder on the theme of the meaning and purpose of creation, this ground of faith in immortality is, perhaps, the most broadly satisfactory of any. Having once learned to think of God as the almighty Guide, who is leading every soul he has made to the joy of eternal union with himself, it becomes simply impossible to lower that conception, and think of him as content to "let him that is unjust be unjust still," and permit his rebellious child to perish forever with a blasphemy on his lips.

III. Again: the incompleteness and imperfection of the noblest part of man, compared to the finished work which creation elsewhere presents, affords ground for the presumption that that noblest part has not yet reached the development it is intended to attain. The green leaf gives no promise of becoming any thing but a leaf; and in due time it withers, and drops to the ground, without exciting in the beholder any sense of disappointment. But the flower-bud holds out a different prospect. If the canker-worm devour it ere it bloom into a rose, we are sensible of grievous failure; and a garden in which all the buds should so perish would be more hideous than any desert. The body of a man grows to its full stature and complete development; but no man has ever yet reached his loftiest mental stature, or the plenitude of moral strength and beauty of which he is capable. If the simile be just which compares the physical nature to a scaffolding, and the spiritual to the temple built up within it, then we behold the strange anomaly of a mere framework made so perfect, that it could gain nothing, were it preserved to the fabulous age of the patriarchs; while the temple within is never finished, and is often an unsightly heap. The "City of God" cannot be built of piles never to be completed, nor his garden of souls filled with flowers destined all to canker ere they bloom.

IV. Human love also urges on us an appeal to faith, which has probably been to millions of hearts the most conclusive of all. We are fond of quoting the assertion, that

> "'Tis better to have loved and lost
> Than never to have loved at all."

But its truth may very much be questioned, unless we can trust that the "many waters" of the dark river "cannot quench love," and that we shall surely rejoice still in that light of life upon the farther shore. Intense love becomes torture, if we believe it to be a transient joy, the "meteor gleam of a starless night," and fear that it must soon go out in unfathomable gloom. To think of the one whose innermost self is to us the world's chief treasure, the most beautiful and blessed thing God ever made, and believe that at any moment that mind and heart may cease to *be*, and become only a memory, every noble gift and grace extinct, and all the fond love for ourselves forgotten forever, — this is such agony, that, having once known it, we should never dare again to open our hearts to affection, unless some ray of hope should dawn for us beyond the grave. Love would be the curse of mortality, were it to bring always with it such unutterable pain of anxiety, and the knowledge that every hour which knitted our heart more closely to our friend, also brought us nearer to an eternal separation. Better never to have ascended to that high *Vita Nuova* where self-love is lost in another's weal, better to have lived like the cattle, which browse and sleep while they wait the butcher's knife, than to endure such despair.

But is there nothing in us which refuses to believe all this nightmare of the final sundering of loving hearts? Love itself seems to announce itself as an eternal thing. It has such an element of infinity in its tenderness, that it never fails to seek for itself an expression beyond the limits of time; and we talk, even when we know not what we mean, of "undying affection," "immortal love." It is the only passion, which, in the nature of things, we can carry with us into another world; and it is fit to be prolonged, intensified, glorified forever. It is not so much a joy we *may* take with us, as the only joy which can make any world a heaven when the affections of earth shall be perfected in the supreme love of God. It is the sentiment which we share with God, and by which we live in him, and he in us. All its beautiful tenderness, its noble self-forgetfulness, its pure and ineffable delight, are the rays of God's sun of love reflected in our souls.

Is all this to end in two poor heaps of silent dust decaying slowly in their coffins side by side in the vault? If so, let us have done with prating of any faith in heaven or earth. We are mocked by a fiend. Mephistopheles is on the throne of the universe.

V. Another and very remarkable moral argument for immortality was put forth some years ago by Prof. Newman, and has never (to my knowledge) attracted the attention it deserves.

It cannot be stated more succinctly than in his own volume of "Theism" (p. 75). After describing our pain at the loss of a friend, he continues, —

"But if virtue grieve thus for lost virtue justly,
How, then, must God, the fountain of virtue, feel?
If our highest feelings, and the feelings of all the holy,
Guide rightly to the divine heart, then it would grieve likewise,
And grieve eternally, if goodness perish eternally.
Nay, and as a man who should live ten thousand years,
Sustained miraculously amid perishing generations,
Would sorrow perpetually in the perpetual loss of friends,
Even so some might judge the divine heart likewise
Would stint its affections towards the creatures of a day. . . .
Would it not be a yawning gulf of ever-increasing sorrow
Losing every loved one just when virtue was ripening,
And foreseeing perpetual loss, friend after friend, forever,
So that all training perishes, and has to be begun anew,
Winning new souls to virtue, to be lost as soon as won?
If, then, we must not doubt that the Highest has deep love for the holy,
Such love as man has for man in pure and sacred friendship,
We seem justly to infer that those whom God loves are deathless;
Else would the divine blessedness be imperfect and impaired.
Nor avails it to reply by resting on God's infinitude,
Which easily supports sorrows which would weigh us down;

For if to promote virtue be the highest end with the
Creator,
Then to lose his own work, not casually and by exception,
But necessarily and always, agrees not with his infinitude
More than with his wisdom, nor more than with his
blessedness.
In short, close friendship between the Eternal and the
perishing
Appears unseemly to the nature of the Eternal,
Whom it befits to keep his beloved, or not to love at all.
But to say God loveth no man is to make religion vain:
Hence it is judged that 'whatsoever God loveth liveth
with God.'"

In the five ways now specified, the moral arguments drawn from the phenomena of human life and sentiment, and from all that we may conjecture of the divine purposes, lead up indirectly to the conclusion that there must be another act of the drama after that on which the curtain falls at death.

There remain some other lines of thought, converging towards the same end, which cannot now be followed out; as, for example, the ennobling influence of the belief in immortality, which faith refuses to trace to a delusion. Space only can be reserved to touch briefly on the two forms in which mankind possesses something like a *direct* consciousness of a life after death, and in which faith therefore, speaks, immediately, and without any preliminary argument. These two forms are, 1st, The general dim consciousness of the mass of mankind, that the soul of a man never dies; 2d, The specific vivid consciousness of devout men, that their spiritual union with God is eternal.

VI. The first of these forms of direct faith is too familiar a topic to need much elucidation. The extreme variability of its manifestations in nations and individuals makes it difficult to estimate its just value, and to decide whether we have a right to treat it as a mere tradition, or as the *quasi*-universal testimony of the soul to its own natural superiority to death. It may be remarked, however, that the belief, when examined carefully (e.g., as in Alger's admirable "History of the Doctrine of a Future Life"), bears very much the characteristics we should attribute to a real and spontaneous instinct, and not to any common tradition, such as that of a deluge, disseminated by the various branches of the human family in their migrations. 1st, The belief begins early, though, probably, not in the very earliest stage of human development; 2d, It attains its maximum among the highest races of mankind, in the great primary forms of civilization (e.g., the Egyptian, Vedic-Aryan, and Persian); 3d, It projects such various and even contrasted ideals of the future world (e.g., Valhalla and Nirvana), that it must be supposed to have sprung up indigenously in each race, and by no means to have been borrowed by one from the other; 4th, Finally, the instinct begins to falter at a later stage of civilization, when self-consciousness is more developed, and the practice of arguing about our beliefs takes the place of more simple habits of mind, — a stage which we may, perhaps, exactly mark in Roman history, when, as Cicero tells us, "there were some in his day who had begun to doubt of immortality." All these characters would certainly form "notes" of an original instinct in the human soul, testifying to its own undyingness, and are not easily accounted for on any other hypothesis.

It will be observed that this consciousness of immortality, and the expectation of justice, spoken of above, are entirely distinct things. Though confluent at last, they have remote sources. It is at a comparatively late stage of history, that the expectation of justice projects itself beyond the horizon of this world, and at an equally late one when the consciousness of immortality crystallizes into a definite idea of a state of rewards and punishments.

Direct reliance on this consciousness of immortality, when it happens to be strongly developed in the individual, is probably the origin of that robust faith which we still find, not rarely, among persons of warm and simple natures. Those amongst us who lack such vivid instinct may yet obtain, indirectly, a ground of confidence from the observation of its almost universal prevalence, implying its divine origin and consequent veracity. That the Creator of the human race should have so formed our mental constitution as that such a belief should have sprung up, and prevailed over the whole globe, and yet that it should be, from first to last, a mistake, is an hypothesis which faith cannot endure. The God of truth will have deceived the human race, if the soul of a man dies with his body.

VII. Lastly: the most perfect and direct faith in immortality is assuredly that which is vouchsafed to the happy souls who personally feel that they have entered into a relation with God, which can never end. It is hard to speak on this sacred theme without appearing to some irreverent, to others fanatical. I can but say that there are men and women who have given their testimony in this matter whom I think we do well to trust, even as prophets who have stood on Pisgah. "Faith in God and in our eternal union with him," said one of them, "are not two dogmas of our creed, but one." That inner experience which is the living knowledge of the one truth brings home also the other. At a certain stage of religious progress, we cannot doubt that the man learns by direct perception that God loves him, and that "he is in God, and God in him," in a sense which conveys the warrant of eternal life. As humbler souls find their last word of faith to be that of Marcus Aurelius, — "Thou wilt do well for me and for the world," — such a man has the loftier right to say with assurance, "Thou wilt guide me by thy counsel, and afterwards receive me to glory. Thou wilt not leave my soul in hell, nor suffer thine holy one to see corruption."

Perhaps the knowledge of his immortality has come to the saint in some supreme hour of adoring happiness. Perhaps it has come when the clouds of death seemed to close round him, and, instead of darkness, lo! there was a great light, and a sense of life flowing fresh and strong against the ebbing tide of mortality; a life which is the same as love, the same as infinite joy and trust. It matters not whence or how it came. Thenceforth there is for him no more doubt. The next world is as sure as the present, and God is shining over all.

Such, for a few blessed souls, seems to be the perfect "evidence of things not seen." But can their full faith supply our lack? Can we see with their eyes, and believe on their report? It is only possible in a very inferior measure. Yet if our own spiritual life have received even some faint gleams of the "light which never came from sun or star," then once more will our faith point the way to immortality; for we shall know in what manner such truths come to the soul, and be able to trust that what is dawn to us may be sunrise to those who have journeyed nearer to the east than we; who have surmounted duty more perfectly, or passed through rivers of affliction into which our feet have never dipped. God cannot have deluded them in their sacred hope of his eternal love. If their experience be a dream, all prayer and all communion may likewise be dreams. In so far as we have faith in such prayer and communion, we can believe in the high experience of the saints, and so in the immortal life to which it witnesses.

II.

THE immense growth which has taken place in the moral consciousness of mankind within historical times may be estimated by a simple observation. The future life, which was once altogether uncolored by moral hues, has, for ages, been painted as if it were a moral life only — all its happiness, reward; and all its suffering, either retribution or purification. In the preceding paper, it was remarked, in passing, that the consciousness of immortality, and the expectation of justice, are totally distinct things, and, though confluent at last, arise in remote sources. It is at a comparatively late historical era that the expectation of justice projects itself beyond the horizon of this world, and equally late when the consciousness of immortality takes shape as an ideal state of rewards and punishments beyond the grave. But, having once passed into this phase, it is astonishing how rapidly our moral aspect of the future world begins to occupy the minds of men, almost to the exclusion of every other. The analogies of the present existence (if they might be accounted in any measure as guides) would lead us to infer that hereafter, as here, the moral life will be only one of the elements of existence, and, though the most important of all (and therefore more discernible at a higher elevation), yet never absolutely bare and alone, but rather, like the granite foundations of the eternal hills, clothed with forests of usefulness, and flowery meads of beauty and affection. Instead of this, the popular idea for millenniums has been, that, the moment a man dies, he goes, *not* into a higher school with its lessons and its play (often the most instructive of lessons), but into a divine police-court, where the presiding magistrate — Minos or Osiris, or he who frowns behind the altar of the Sistine — is always sitting in readiness to send him to the dread prison on one hand, or to dole him out the arrears of pay for his faith and virtues on the other. When that sentence has been passed, all that follows throughout eternity is (according to the same conception) merely a sequel thereof, — either punishment or reward, under different forms of suffering or enjoyment.

Of course, among persons accustomed to think freely for themselves, such views as these carry no authority; but it would be well, if, before turning our attention to a study of the problems connected with the possible conditions of a future life, we could shake ourselves altogether free of them, and start afresh. That which the past has really bequeathed to us is an immense *consensus* of the human race in favor of the two opinions, "that the soul of a man never dies," and that "justice will be done hereafter, if not here." The value of this almost universal testimony is (as I have endeavored to show in the preceding part of this essay) very great indeed. But, beyond these two great general affirmations, the voice of the ages can say nothing to us of the smallest weight concerning either the details of the life to come, or of the special form in which justice is to be fulfilled. The soul may have consciousness of its own immortality; and the moral sense may point to the final triumph of justice, as the needle points to the magnetic pole: but the details of how, when, and where, the future life is to be spent, or how justice is to be fulfilled, are matters regarding which it is impossible that we can have any consciousness; and such ideas as we inherit concerning them must needs have come to us through the exercise of the mythopœic faculty of men of old, elevated, as time went on, to the rank of divine revelations. And it is to be remarked, that as these ideas (e.g., that of a New Jerusalem) were evolved in accordance with the psychology, politics, æsthetics, and all other conditions of the community which gave them birth, so they inevitably bear the stamp of their age; and we entangle ourselves in endless anachronisms by retaining them now, even with widest latitude of Swedenborgian type-making. Few readers of Gibbon will forget the scorn wherewith that

"Lord of irony, the master-spell
Which stung his foes to hate which grew from fear,"

describes the origin of the Apocalyptic vision. In the state of society in the Roman empire in the first and second centuries, a town was the centre of all delights, and the country was considered a place of banishment. "A city," he says, "was accordingly constructed in the skies of gold and jewels." Now in England, on the contrary, in the nineteenth century, nothing can be further from our notions of peace and repose than a walled town, even if provided with gates of the singularly incongruous material of pearls. Rather, when Martin, some years ago, desired to paint the "Plains of Heaven," he innocently sketched a handsome English pleasure-ground, with a distant view, — let us say of the Weald of Kent, or of the Shropshire woodlands with the Welsh mountains in the horizon. Had he attempted to depict the blessed walking up and down on the *trottoirs* of a gold-paved street, his critics would have treated him as a caricaturist of the legend of Whittington, rather than as an illustrator of the Vision of the Seer of Patmos. And yet it may be questioned, whether, in the minds of thousands amongst us, orthodox and heterodox, some dim idea of the Apocalyptic city does not even yet arise whenever we think of another life, — an idea, perhaps, more directly derived, in our case, from Bunyan than from St. John. It would be superfluous to remark further, how the doctrine of the resurrection of the body, which accommodated itself to the pneumatology of the Egyptians and Jewish Pharisee, still colors the notions of persons who have (so far as they are conscious) entirely renounced any such belief, and who are quite aware of the insolubility of the problems concerning spirit and matter, of which the ancients cut the knot with so much decision. If we would avoid following in the wake of perfectly unseaworthy speculations, we must needs let all these notions drift away from us at once and forever.

Another order of errors, from which it is also very desirable we should clear our minds, are those which arise from the old view of the Creator as a *Deus ex machina*, always ready miraculously to interfere with the order of things, and bring his moral will suddenly to bear upon and snap the chain of physical events. If the soul does, as we believe, survive the dissolution of the body, then that survival is assuredly a *natural* event, prepared for, even from the first beginnings of our physical existence, and taking place normally as the new-born child enters the world. The child comes into the light out of darkness, and we seem to pass into darkness out of light; but the one transition must be as natural as the other. It is among the "infinite possibilities of Nature," — Nature, whose laws are the changeless habits of God, — that the immortality of the human soul must be henceforth anticipated, not among the beneficent freaks of an erratic Omnipotence.

Excluding these ancient misleadings, and endeavoring to stand face to face with the bare fact that the self of man must be disembodied, if it survive death, what are the conditions of existence conceivable under such severance? It is a truism all too familiar, that an unborn babe might prophesy of the flowers and stars which are shortly to meet its eyes, as well as a living man tell of the things which lie beyond the tomb. But I apprehend that the utter, unilluminable darkness which conceals the whole *outer* environment of the future life (a darkness which no apocalypse could lighten) does not close quite so impenetrably as has been generally supposed over the conditions of the *inner* world which we must needs carry with us. Our position is, in a measure, like that of a blind man who should be told, that, on a certain day, he should both receive his sight, and suffer amputation of his arms. What receiving his sight may be, he cannot in the remotest degree guess or understand; but he may form some, not wholly false, conception of what it will be to lose his limbs. At death, a portcullis falls on the senses, the appetites are cut off at their roots, and the affections are subjected to a strain of changed conditions hitherto untried. Perhaps still more intimate changes may be involved; and, with the loss of its brain-tablet, memory may alter its character. In any case, our whole past world is gone, whatever new one may, either immediately or at a remoter future, take its place, and supply us with fresh sensations and ideas. Like creatures which have hitherto inhabited the waters, we quit the element in which we have lived and moved and had our being; and whatever we have henceforth to experience must come from another. Yet we carry *ourselves* into the new element, — selves which must be affected most importantly by the transition, but which cannot, in the nature of things, lose their individuality, or change instantaneously their ethical status. In the following pages, regard will be paid exclusively to those problems which arise on contemplating the simple fact of disembodiment and its consequences; and no attempt whatever will be made to construct any theory of the *outward* conditions of the surviving self, or its possible environment. Further, it must be understood that it is rather with the hope of stating such problems with some fresh clearness, and leaving the reader to choose between the dilemmas which arise, than with the bolder ambition of offering a solution of them, that I have engaged in this task. Only in a few cases has it seemed to me that there are indications sufficiently obvious to enable us to decide with some degree of confidence regarding the true answers to the eager questions of our hearts. To avoid perpetual circumlocutions, I shall speak generally of the disembodied self as the "soul," without thereby intending to commit myself to any particular theory associated with the word, either as distinguished from matter or (according to the ancient pneumatology) from that much-misleading term, "spirit."[1]

I. With regard to the intellectual part of us, which may survive dissolution, the difficulties seem even more abstruse and insoluble than those which concern the love which may be

[1] It may, perhaps, aid a little to bring reader and writer to mutual comprehension in these obscure researches, if I say that such idea as I have been able to form of the *rationale* of immortality is, that life, vegetative, animated, conscious, and self-conscious, forms a series of evolutions, not merely in the sense of a higher and more elaborate organization, but of a subtler essence, — a series of sheaths, out of which finer and finer shoots grow successively, till at last comes the flower of full consciousness, into whose heart the divine sun pours his beams directly, and wherein is formed a seed which does not perish when the petals fall in the dust. The stage of being at which *something*, self-conscious or otherwise, survives the dissolution of the body may be — nay (in my humble opinion), is almost certainly — a lower one than we have been accustomed to consider. A few only out of the grounds of faith in human immortality apply to the immortality of the higher brutes; but *human immortality being assumed as a given fact*, and a future life for man being predicated as *normal*, the physiological laws (whatever they may be) under which such survival takes place in our case are almost sure to apply to creatures many of whom possess intelligence and sentiment far surpassing those of human infants. The great argument of justice, of course, applies to ill-used and innocent beasts with even greater force than to similarly ill-used but more or less guilty men.

renewed, or the justice which may be fulfilled hereafter. Is knowledge such as we gain on earth an everlasting treasure? Can we lose it any more than we can lose the food which we have swallowed, and which has gone to make up the tissue of our frames? Or, on the other hand, can we keep it, and carry it with us, entering the higher state, one of us as a philosopher, and the other as a boor? If this last hypothesis be the nearest to the truth, then we ask, Whether all kinds of knowledge, or only the knowledge which deals with Nature or eternal things, have value in the other world? Thus we find ourselves conducted to the practical query, Whether the education of earth ought not to be carried on with reference to the probable value of mental acquirements beyond the sphere of human concerns? The common and orthodox notion of immortality seems to be, that the silliest or most ignorant person, admitted into heaven, instantly becomes wiser than Plato, and far better acquainted with science than Humboldt. But even new organs, new capacities, new revelations, can scarcely convey such knowledge and wisdom *instantaneously*. The philosopher who has eagerly sought some hidden truth may find the light immediately break on his soul; the man of science, who has thoroughly understood, and ardently endeavored to untie, the knots of creation's mysteries, may be enabled to loosen them by the help of fresh faculties and wider vision: but it seems well-nigh nonsense to talk of a clown, who has no notion that there are hidden truths or mysteries waiting explanation, receiving the whole flood of *quasi*-omniscience into the narrow mill-dam of his soul. "To him that hath shall be given." For him that hath not, some rudiments and dawning rays of knowledge seem all that he is capable of receiving. The Hottentot who died in his *kraal* an hour before Sir John Herschel, did he learn in that hour more about the laws and motions of the heavenly bodies than Herschel knew? Or were Herschel's illumined eyes able to take in at a glance what the Hottentot will take years to learn, when, as the old Greek epitaph on Thales has it, "He was removed on high because his eyes, dimmed by age, could no longer from afar behold the stars"?

The difficulty of conceiving how any mental act is hereafter to be performed *without* a brain, which hitherto has been performed,—if not "*by*," yet invariably "*with*" and "*through*," the brain,—has been, undoubtedly, immeasurably heightened by recent physiological discoveries, which have tended more and more at each step to connect both thought and memory with changes in cerebral matter. Dr. Carpenter's very remarkable paper in "The Contemporary Review" for May, 1873, "On the Hereditary Transmission of Acquired Psychical Habits," goes very far indeed towards identifying alike the consciousness of present sensorial impressions and the memory of past ones, with physical changes in the brain; and however willing we may be to retain the notion that there is a soul in all cases (except, perhaps, those of unconscious or involuntary cerebration), present and active, using the brain as its instrument, and no more identifiable therewith than the organist with his organ, we still find ourselves face to face with an appalling problem, when we try to imagine any way in which a brainless soul can think or remember. The two hypotheses open to us in the matter are, to suppose either, first, that the thing which we speak of as the soul has many powers undisclosed now, while it is wrapped in the sheath of the body, — powers to perceive (as magnetized persons have been supposed to do) without use of eyes or ears, and corresponding powers to remember without a note-book brain; or, second, that (as Leibnitz insisted with regard to every finite intelligence) the soul is necessarily always clothed with a material body more or less rarefied, and that it finds in its future "spiritual body" of the old Pauline type fresh organs of consciousness. Of these abysses of speculation, the present writer has no intention to do more than skirt the edge, merely refusing to cover them up, as is too often done, with cut-and-dried phrases, like traps awaiting us in the hours of doubt and darkness. The strain on moral and religious faith caused by the difficulties attendant on every theory of a life after death is simply enormous; and, the more plainly we recognize that it is so, the safer we are. He is a foolish engineer who refuses to test, lest it should break down under the strain, the strength of the bridge over which, ere long, every thing dear to him must pass. One point, however, regarding these solemn problems may, I think, here be justly noted, having, in effect, come out into much clearer light than heretofore, in consequence of the physiological discoveries above mentioned. The hypothesis of a re-clothing of the disembodied soul with a new body is now the less tenable of the two, unless we are prepared to anticipate an obliteration of memory. It will not suffice to believe that fresh senses may be developed in a future frame. Such senses might properly reveal to us our future surroundings, as our present ones reveal those which are now present. But it is not conceivable that they should reveal the past; and, if the memorial tablet of the brain be lost, it would appear that we must needs find our new organ of thought a *tabula rasa.* Thus we are shut up in the dilemma, that either the soul carries its own memory with it (in which case it would seem as if it may as naturally retain all other faculties, and so need no fresh body), or that it does *not* carry its memory, and so, when re-embodied, lives beyond Lethe, utterly unaware of what has passed in this state of existence. I am not disposed to insist that there could be absolutely *no* fulfilment of justice, no satisfaction of the unquenched thirst of love, in a world between which and our own had fallen a veil of oblivion. The consequences of our acts (as I shall by and by attempt to show) may bring about sure retribution by working themselves into the very tissue of our souls; and love may draw once more together, and perfect the friendship of spirits whose affinity first proclaimed itself here below. But, undoubtedly, so far as we can yet grasp such thoughts, the retention or restoration of memory is almost, if not absolutely, a *sine qua non* among the conditions of such a life after death as shall altogether fulfil those aspirations which (God-given as we believe them to be) are our chief pledge that such a life awaits us.

II. Very interesting, though less important, are the speculations regarding another world, which refer to that side of our intellectual nature which we call the æsthetic. How will the beauty of our new habitations touch us? Or will it be the yet unexplored loveliness of our own planet which we shall behold at last, and no longer with careworn hearts or tear-dimmed eyes? To how many of the sick and suffering, the narrow-fortuned, the toil-enslaved, have the scenes of Alps and Andes, Grecian Isles and Yosemite Valleys, been dreams of longing never appeased ere death closed their unsatisfied eyes? What bliss might be given to many of the purest of souls, who have passed whole years imprisoned in sordid streets, or amid all the ugliness of a sick-chamber, by merely permitting them "to see those things which we see," of woods and hills and waters, the sunrise and the moon walking in glory amid the clouds? We dare not say it is a debt owing to such souls that they should one day behold God's beautiful world; but assuredly it would be no improbable display of his love to show it to them.

All these questions, however, and all which concern the mental faculties in another life, are (as I said a few pages back) even more rebuffing to our poor thoughts and speculations than those which concern the future of the affections and the conscience; and to these I hasten, as also infinitely the most interesting.

III. If there be a life after death, it can scarcely be but that love will assume therein a much higher place than it holds here. What gifts of tongues and prophecy may cease, what wit and learning and science may "vanish away," we cannot define; but that love "never faileth" is no less sure than that we ourselves shall continue to be. God *cannot*, — it is reverence itself that makes us say it, — God cannot have made our human hearts as if expressly to contain and feed that light of a world else so dark, and yet permit the gleam to be extinguished like the toy-lamps launched on the Ganges, leaving them to go down the stream of eternity in the blackness of night. If he can and does so ordain it, he is not the God who has given us the law of justice and fidelity, nor the adored, all-merciful One whom we have found in life's supremest hours in the Holy of holies of prayer. He is not *our* God; and even if he (or it?) be a "Stream of Tendency," an "Universum," or the "Deity of the Religion of Inhumanity," which our various new teachers would have us recognize, religion is evermore closed to us; for we cannot love him, and the hope of immortality vanishes as a dream. As Florence Nightingale recently wrote, "Our ground for believing in a future life is simply *because God is.*" His character is the pledge of our immortality, and it is quite as much the pledge that the love, which is the most godlike thing in us, shall be immortal too. Our divines are so jealous of what they have deemed to be God's "glory" as the Judge of all the earth, that they have supposed judging to be altogether his chief concern, and that he calls us from the grave expressly to punish us or to reward. But, beside these royal functions of Deity (if we may so express it), there must remain the cares of the tender Father, the divine Friend; and it would be strange indeed, if these should not be vindicated by that good One quite as surely and perfectly as the others.

One of the many questions which crowd on

us, when we attempt to construct any theory of what the future of the affections may be, has, doubtless, made the hearts of the bereaved ache whenever it has occurred to them. What warrant have we, that dying long years after our lost ones, perchance in wholly different spiritual and moral conditions, we shall ever meet or overtake them, and not, rather, remain "evermore a life behind," "through all the secular to be"? Even granting that they live, and we live, who has told us that our paths, which happened to approach, like those of a comet and a planet, for the mere moment of earthly existence, will ever touch again throughout the cycles of eternity? In view of these agonizing questions, we can scarcely wonder at those who have killed themselves with their beloved ones, rather than allow them to go out alone into the darkness, striving thus to secure a *natural* proximity, even while they madly placed the *moral* distance of a great crime between them. The supreme kindness of Providence would seem to be shown, when it suffers two loving spirits to pass linked in inseparable embrace through the awful portals of the unknown world. Could we anticipate such a lot with certainty, death would lose half its terrors and all its sadness.

And again: another painful doubt is, How

shall we recognize our friends in a disembodied or re-embodied state? Suppose that we both live again and meet again, how shall we be sure, that in some strange, glorified form, which passes us by all unwittingly and unrecognized, we shall not miss the being whom we would traverse half eternity to find? These are the anxious, but, after all, somewhat childish, questions which the restlessness of severed affection naturally suggests. But, in truth, we are quite as sure of re-union with our beloved ones, and of mutual recognition, as of the immortal life itself. As we have just observed, the ground of our belief in that life is the same which guarantees the restoration of love, and therefore, implicitly, some sure method of re-union. How it is to be brought about is the concern of Him who will lead us into that unseen land partly for that very purpose. Perhaps we may most readily conceive of it by supposing (what is, for all other reasons, most probable), that, in another life, we shall be indefinitely more *free* than we are now, more able to move and to communicate through space, and having, perhaps, no physical wants, be at length disinthralled from the endless Liliputian cords which bind us here, and often keep apart the tenderest friends. And again: as to the mutual recognition of departed spirits, the question really is not, How should we know, but, How should we *not* know, the one who has been soul of our soul, in any form, or in formless spiritual existence? Even through the thick veil of the flesh, we are always dimly conscious of the presence of love. One sympathizing heart amid a crowd of enemies makes itself felt, and gives strength unspeakable. To suppose that we could ever, at any time, be brought into contact with the spirit which has been nearest to our own, and not recognize it under any disguise, is wholly gratuitously to doubt our instincts. But why should we even postulate that a disguise of any kind is to be anticipated? If the spirit wear any frame, however ethereal, it must bear some resemblance to the first, since both were the fitting shell of the same soul. Such a portrait as Titian made of a man may well stand forever at once for the glorified image of what he was on earth, and the faint and imperfect adumbration of what he is in heaven. Our pitiful grief for

"The garments by the soul laid by,"

which we have placed folded upon the narrow shelves of the tomb, the agony with which we have thought of the grave-damp marring what was so beautiful and so dear, will be soothed, perchance, at last, when we behold the yet lovelier raiment of the same beloved soul, alike in all that we loved so fondly, unlike, inasmuch as every token of weakness and pain and age and care will forever have disappeared.

Again: there are problems of another kind which sometimes cloud the hopes of renewed affection in another world. How, for example, are we to reconcile the conflicting claims of relatives and friends whom we have loved, each supremely in his turn, but who now await us together in the "land of the leal"? Supposing there has been no failure of fidelity, but only that, as the years flowed on, the love of the parent, over whose grave the grass has many times sprung and withered, has been replaced (so far as one affection ever replaces another, which is but little) by the love of a child; and, as friends have drifted away, new attachments have caught the tendrils of our hearts; and, when the wife or husband of youth has long left the earth, we have formed new ties no less sacred and near? It is a part of the beneficent order of things, that such transitions should take place; and, looking back over life, it is impossible, without ruthless violence to ourselves, to give the preference to one over the other, or to be willing to renounce one for the other. If the love of youth were more vehement, that of middle life is more strong: sweet as were the affections of early years, still more tender and grave and noble are the friendships of age. But how is it possible for us to renew simultaneously these relations which followed each other successively? This is the old Sadducean question under a more refined form; and the answer, that "in heaven there is neither marrying, nor giving in marriage," is as little satisfactory a solution to us as it can have been to the disciples of Antigonus. The later doubt, as well as the earlier, seems to have sprung out of the same inveterate propensity for transferring the limitations and negations, as well as the affirmations, of this life, to a higher sphere. Why is it we cannot love *now* many friends with equal intensity? It is only because we are so limited, our time and thoughts are so bounded, and (what is far worse) our hearts are so cold and narrow, that even when we recognize that A, B, and C are all deserving of our uttermost love, we must needs make one supreme, and give the others only the residue of our tenderness and remembrance. This is the true *rationale* of the limits of love on earth; and those who treat them as if they were in themselves good and desirable things, and who would prefer to give or receive only a narrow and exclusive affection, have hardly yet learned the real sense of unselfish attachment.

> "That love for one, from which there doth not spring
> True love for all, is but a worthless thing."[1]

But in a state of existence in which we should be altogether nobler, larger, wider-hearted, and pressed on no longer by the endless claims which break up our present time into fragments, could we not, also, love more than we do now? Relieved from fears of wretched jealousies, with the cycles of immortality before us, and with the whole scope of our natures widened, what should hinder but that we should be able in the same happy hearts to hold at once the love of all whom we have ever loved truly on earth, ay, and of new friends found in heaven? Even conjugal love, fitting and inevitable as it is that there should be exclusiveness in it now, may be as tender hereafter, though no longer passionate, when the wife meets again the husband, whom, in dying, she prayed should find another to love him as well. She will not be less generous there than here; nor will the bitter thought that affection given to another is robbed from

[1] Mrs. Browning's Sonnets.

ourselves prevail more in such connections hereafter than it does now in happy households where the children love the parents the more because they love each and all, and where the father's and mother's hearts have widened with every child born to their arms.

Yet no one can seriously believe, on reflection (what many assume without it), that the next life will be occupied by a continual return upon the present. It cannot be that all our earthly friendships and acquaintances will be renewed, or that every one with whom we have had a few moments' intercourse in the course of our threescore years and ten will certainly meet us again hereafter. Such re-unions would be, in thousands of cases, wholly purposeless; and only the old, narrow heaven could be imagined to secure such an end. Where will the line be drawn, if we are sure to meet some, and by no means sure to meet others? The answer is hard to find; yet I think two obvious principles must prevail. One is the liberty of which we have spoken, the freedom of the disembodied soul to seek out its own affinities in the spiritual world; and the other is the moral necessity which will be laid on us to redeem the unatoned offences and shortcomings of earth towards those from whom we have parted in any thing short of right relations. It could be no realm of peace to many of us, if we could not at last say those words, "Forgive me," which have been on our lips ever since the hour when we learned that the doors of the grave had closed between us and one whom we had wronged, miscontrued, failed to love as he deserved.

> "The right ear which is filled with dust
> Hears little of the true or just."

But if we could not hope to speak hereafter, "spirit to spirit, ghost to ghost," and let the dead know all our repentance, immortality would cease to represent the completion of the web of existence. Some of the threads which we most desire to take up would remain forever ravelled. And we, too, for our share, must receive the atonements of love and regret for the pangs which unkindness, mistrust, moroseness, and perchance cruelty, have given us, from the unjust severity and repression which crushed the joy of childhood, to the last neglect of tedious age. Not necessarily or even probably need there be any revision of special acts, only (what we need so sorely) the admission that the wrongs done to us are felt to have been wrongs indeed, and the establishment evermore of truer and more just relations. These reflections belong more properly to the succeeding portion of this paper, wherein the moral state of departed souls will be considered; but I cannot but add one word here of the overwhelming impressiveness of the view opened to us through such a conception of justice as this. Not by the arbitrary sentence of an omnipotent Judge, dismissing the persecutor to the dungeons of hell, and seating the martyr on the thrones of paradise, would our highest thought be fulfilled, while the damned one should forever curse and hate, and the glorified know that he had an enemy even in the nethermost vaults of death. Only by the subduing of the heart of the wrong-doer, the vanquishing not of *him*, but of his hate, and the melting of his spirit in remorse and penitence at the feet of his victim, can we conceive of the fitting close of the awful drama. The penitence of an enemy, which shall be his salvation as well as his atonement to us — *that* we may accept with solemn joy, even when risen a hundred-fold nearer to God than we are now; but his physical torture, "where the worm dieth not, and the fire is not quenched" — *that* we could not endure, even were we to remain poor and imperfect human creatures still. All the glory of the skies would be blackened by the smoke of the pit, and through the anthems of the archangels our ears would catch the discord of the wail of the lost.

In brief, then, the persons with whom we may confidently expect to have relationships in the world to come are, —

1. Those whom we have loved.
2. Those whom we have hated.
3. Those who have hated us.

I leave the reader to draw the very obvious conclusions regarding the influence which such expectations ought to have upon our present feelings. To look on those whom we love as *ours forever* — ours in a purer sphere than this — is to ennoble and sanctify our love. To look on those whom we hate, or on those who hate us, as beings with whom, some day or other, we *must* be reconciled, is to deprive hatred of its sting, and almost to transform it into love.

But admitting that our hearts, in another life, may be wide enough to gather into them every affection of the past at once, it would still seem hard to guess how the natural ties of our human nature will bind us hereafter. There are friendships which seem obviously made for an eternal world, which have had their roots in religious sympathies or the interchange of moral help, and which would scarcely need any modification to be transferred to the spiritual realms. They have been a part of our heaven always. But, on the other hand, there are affections, if not more tender, yet more human, than these, which, when they are severed by death, seem almost irreparably snapped asunder. We and the departed may meet again as spirits in a world of spirits, but never more (so our hearts moan in their despair), — never more as mother and child, son and father, husband and wife. All the infinite sweetness of those purely human ties seems as if it must exhale, and be lost, when the last act of mortal companionship has been accomplished, and the kindred dust has been laid side by side. And yet *need* we be so sure it is so? Are not our thoughts of these temples of flesh, wherein God has caused us to dwell, far too little reverent, and too much tinged, even yet, with the old gnostic notions of the impurity of matter, the unholiness of Nature, which have pervaded all post-Pauline Christianity? I cannot but think that it is in a true direction modern sentiment is growing, while it tends continually to dignify and hallow the body, and to find infinite beauty and sacredness in the relations which spring out of its mysterious laws. So long as men and women deemed themselves holier as celibates than as husbands and wives, and that the laws of Nature were supposed to have been set aside to give Christ an immaculate mother (as if natural motherhood were not the divinest thing God has made), — so long as this was the case, it was inevitable that the bonds of consanguinity should be supposed to be finally unloosed by death. But with other thoughts of our sacred human rights, of all the depth of meaning which lies (rarely half fathomed here) in the names of father and mother, brother and sister, husband and wife, son and daughter, shall we have no hope, that, when our spirits meet again, it will be in such sort as that the old beloved ties shall never be forgotten, but rather, that what fell short in our comprehension and enjoyment of them will yet be made up? It seems to me almost to follow from the very statement of the problem that it must be so.

But *sin?* What can we hope or think of future re-union, when heinous guilt has been incurred on one side or the other? How are relations and friends, once dear to each other, to meet after the revelation of this gulf between their feet?

I confess that it has been with great surprise that I have read the eloquent words on this subject of a distinguished living writer, with whose scheme of theology in general I have almost entire sympathy, and for whose manly honesty, and powerful grasp of thought, I entertain sincere admiration. In speculating on the awful probabilities of "elsewhere," Mr. Greg lays it down, as if it were an obvious truth, that love must retreat from the discovery of the sinfulness of the person hitherto beloved, and that both saint and sinner will accept as inevitable an eternal separation.[1] Further: Mr. Greg thinks it possible, that, at the highest summit of finite existence, the souls which have ascended together through all the shining ranks for half an eternity of angelic friendship will part company at last; thought forever superseding love. "Farewell, we lose ourselves in light." It would perhaps be wrong to say that the two views hang logically together, and that the mind which (with all its capacity to understand and express the tenderest feelings) yet holds that there may even possibly be something more divine than love, may well also imagine that love cannot conquer sin. But is it not only by a strange transposition in the true table of precedence of human faculties that either doctrine can be accepted? Let us

[1] Enigmas, first edition, p. 263.

suppose two persons loving each other genuinely and tenderly in this life (so much is granted in the hypothesis). The very power of the worse to love the better truly and unselfishly is *ipso facto* evidence of his being loveworthy, of his having in him, in the depth of his nature, the kernel of all goodness, the seed out of which all moral beauty springs, and which whosoever sees and recognizes in his brother's soul cannot choose but love. "Spirit," says the Bhagvat Ghita in one of its deepest utterances, — "spirit is always lovely." There is something at the very root of our being, which, when revealed to any other spirit, calls forth spontaneously sympathy and affection. It is because we do not commonly see this innermost core of our fellow-men, because it is hidden under a mass of fleshly lusts and worldly ambitions, or because they cover it up carefully in a thousand folds of artificial and second-hand sentiments, that they are so little interesting to us. But let chance blow aside the mantle for an instant, let us see a human heart in the moment of its supreme joy or agony, remorse or victory, and, hard as the nether mill-stone as our own hearts may be, they will vibrate like the Lia-Fail when the true king stood on it to be crowned. When we conceive of a holy

God loving such creatures as ourselves, it is only by the help of the faith that his eye can see this "lovely spirit" beneath all its coverings and concealments. Whether there exists, or has ever existed, a rational creature of God, in whom there was no such germ of goodness and innermost core of loveliness, it is impossible to say. Hideous tales there are of men, with the hearts of tigers and the brains of murderers, who have passed through childhood and youth without once displaying a trait of infant tenderness or boyish affection, and who seem utterly incapable of understanding what self-sacrificing love may mean. The dog which dies to save his master is a million-fold more *human* than they. What may be the key to the horrible mystery of such lives of moral idiotcy, whether, indeed, they ever really exist in all the deformity which has been painted, and, if so, whether fearful physiological maleformations of brain, and the negation of every good influence in childhood, are not to be held accountable for the monsters' growth, I cannot now argue. But one thing is certain from the very statement of the case: a man who has ever once truly loved *anybody* is no such creature. The poor, self-condemned soul whom Mr. Greg images as turning away in an agony of shame and hopelessness from the virtuous friend he loved on earth, and loves still at an immeasurable distance, — such a soul is not outside the pale of love, divine or human. Nay, is he not, even assuming his guilt to be black as night, only in a similar relation to the purest of created souls, which that pure soul holds to the All-Holy One above? If God can love *us*, is it not the acme of moral presumption to think of a human soul being too pure to love *any* sinner, so long as in him there remains any vestige of affection? The whole problem is unreal and impossible. In the first place, there is a potential moral equality between all souls capable of equal love; and the one can never reach a height whence it may justly despise the other. And, in the second place, the higher the virtuous soul may have risen in the spiritual world, the more it must have acquired the godlike insight which beholds the good under the evil, and not less the godlike love which embraces the repentant prodigal.[1]

1 It is with sincere pleasure that I add, on the republication of this paper, the following generous admission and candid revision of his judgment, which Mr. Greg has appended to the last (seventh) edition of his Enigmas of Life. After quoting some observations of the Rev. J. Hamilton Thom and the above, he says, —

But, if such a dream of future separation for loving souls be wholly baseless, what can we imagine of the real relation which may subsist

"The force of these objections to my delineation cannot be gainsaid, and ought not to have been overlooked. No doubt, a soul that can so love, and so feel its separation from the objects of its love, cannot be wholly lost. It must still retain elements of recovery and redemption, and qualities to win and to merit answering affection. The lovingness of a nature, its capacity for strong and deep attachment, must constitute, there as here, the most hopeful characteristic out of which to elicit and foster all other good. No doubt, again, if the sinful continue to love in spite of their sinfulness, the blessed will not cease to love in consequence of their blessedness. If so, it is natural, and indeed inevitable, to infer that a chief portion of their occupation in the spiritual world will consist in comforting the misery, and assisting in the restoration, of the lost whom they have loved. We shall pursue this work with all the aid which our augmented powers on the one side, and their purged perceptions on the other, will combine to gather round the task; and in the success and completion of that task, and in that alone, must lie the consummation of the bliss of heaven.

"But this is not the only, nor perhaps the most irresistible, inference forced upon us by the above considerations. If so vast an ingredient in the misery of the condemned consist in the severance from those they love, this same severance must form a terrible drawback from the felicity of the redeemed. How, indeed, *can* they enjoy any thing to be called happiness hereafter, if the bad — *their* bad, not strangers, but their dearest intimates, those who have shared their inmost confidences, and made up the intensest interests of their earthly life — are groaning and writhing in hopeless anguish close at hand? (for every thing will be close to us in that scene where darkness and distance are no more.) Obviously only in one way, — *by ceasing to love;* that is, by renouncing, or losing, or crushing, the best and purest part of their nature, by abjur-

hereafter between souls attached in faithful friendship, but of which one is of far higher moral standing than the other? It is a very

ing the most specific teaching of Christ, by turning away from the worship and imitation of that God who is love. Or, to put it in still terser and bolder language, how, *given a hell of torment and despair for millions of our friends and fellow-men,* can the good enjoy heaven, except by becoming bad? without becoming transformed, miraculously changed, and *changed deplorably for the worse?* without, in a word, putting on, along with the white garments of the redeemed, a coldness and hardness of heart, a stony, supercilious egotism, which on earth would have justly forfeited all claim to regard, endurance, or esteem? Our affections are probably the best things about us, — the attributes through which we most approach and resemble the divine nature: yet, assuming the hell of theologians, those affections must be foregone or trampled down in heaven, or else heaven will itself become a hell. As a condition, or a consequence, of being admitted to the presence of God, we should have to forswear the little that is godlike in our composition. Do not these simple reflections suffice to disperse into thin air the current notions of a world of everlasting pain?

"One further corollary may be briefly indicated. Hell, if there be such a place or state, though a scene of merited and awful suffering, must be full of the mighty mitigations which hope always brings, and can scarcely be devoid of an element of sweetness which might almost seem like joy, if the consciousness be permitted and ever present to its denizens, that 'elsewhere' guardian angels — parents who have 'entered into glory,' wives who cluster round the throne, sisters and friends who have 'emerged from the ruins of the tomb and the deeper ruins of the fall' — are forever at work, with untiring faithfulness, and the sure instincts of a perfected intelligence, for the purification of the stained, the strengthening of the weak, the softening of the fierce and hard, and the final rescue of them all." — *Postscriptum*, p. 311.

hard thing to conceive how the guilt of a beloved soul would look from the regions of celestial purity; but I think something may be done to help ourselves, if we endeavor to fix our attention steadily on what would probably hold an analogous position in our eyes, namely, the sins of our own long past years. Passing over the mere faults of childhood, many of us can unhappily remember committing very serious errors at a period of youth when we had attained to full responsibility. Looking back to one of these sins, say, after twenty or forty years, how does it strike us? We do not, I apprehend, feel much of the indignation against ourselves which in a certain measure warps our judgment of offences still recent, the disgust of sloughs into which even now we do not feel safe but that our foot again may slip. We can think of the old faults, long lived over or conquered, calmly as of the faults of another person. But it is of another whose inmost mind, and all whose antecedents, are intimately known to us. Very commonly we feel that we deserved the heaviest punishment for our misdeeds; that what did befall us of evil was perfectly merited, and that much heavier chastisement would not have exceeded our deserts. Yet we never feel that we were deserving of *reprobation*, of being finally abandoned by God or man. We say to ourselves, "I was odious at that age. How heartless, self-engrossed, false, sensual, ungenerous, I was! Truly there was hardly a spark of good in me, and I wonder my friends bore me any affection." But, even while we thus condemn ourselves, there is a latent comprehension of how it all came about; how we had slipped into this fault, or been led into that one; found ourselves entangled by a preceding act, and driven into the third; and how, all through, there was, at bottom, the possibility of becoming better, the seed of somewhat which God's kind hand has since planted in a happier soil. Probably few of us turn from such memories save with the thanksgiving of the Psalmist to Him who has taken our feet out of the net, out of the mire and clay, and set them on a rock, and ordered our goings. But, while we bless God for his mercy to our sinfulness, that mercy only seems to us the natural act of a divine Creator who penetrates all the depths of his creature's soul, and with a compassion all-forgiving, because all-knowing, pities and helps our helplessness. The creeds which have taught men that God first gives over his children to a reprobate mind, and then consigns them to a world of reprobation, find nothing to countenance them in the experience of the heart. They teach, strictly speaking, an *unnatural* God. The natural Father-God is a very different Person. Now, in a certain faint and far-off way, we can imagine (not presumptuously, I think) the sympathy of God for the struggling soul to be like that which we should feel for a beloved child whose faults we understood better than any earthly parent, and even better than we understand the faults of our own youth. There is no abatement needful of the full measure of condemnation for the sin. There is only the reservation (never forgotten in our own case) that the sinner was something else besides a sinner, that there were outlying tracts of his nature over which the blight never wholly prevailed; that he was, after all, worth saving. And like this sympathy of God for us in our worst and darkest hours must surely be the sympathy of a glorified soul for its sinful brother. Like him, he must hate the sin which stands revealed in the blaze of heaven in blacker hues than moral realities ever wear in the dim twilight of earth. But, like him, he must feel ineffable tenderness and pity for the spirit wearing that foul stain, and a godlike will to help him to perfect purification. It would not be too much, indeed, to imagine the very converse of the eternal parting of "elsewhere," even the self-losing of the purer soul in its infinite longing for the pardon of the sinful one, and its flight through all the worlds of space, locked in an embrace, not, like Paolo and Francesca's, of a common guilt, but of a common prayer.

And again: at the summit of existence, far up above the clouds and storms of sin and penitence, in the high realm of everlasting peace, will love have no more place? Then the greatness of man must consist in somewhat else than the greatness of God. God has not been content to "lose himself in light," and live alone in his ineffable radiance throughout eternity. He has filled the universe with life and love; and his own awful joy, so far as we may catch the glitter of its sheen, must consist in love, — in loving those whom he blesses, and blessing those whom he loves. Whatever other mysteries of joy are hidden in him, what delight he may take in the beauty of his glorious works, or the rhythmic dance of the clusters of suns, or yet in sources of happiness utterly inconceivable and unknown to us, there must remain, even for him, one joy greater than these, — the joy of infinite love and eternal benediction. As we climb up, age after age, the steps of the interminable ascent, nearer and more like to him,

> "Aloft, aloft, from terrace to broad terrace evermore,"

we must share that joy; and, if we could "lose ourselves" at all, it would rather be in the ocean of love than in the unbreathable ether of a purely intellectual existence. Christ must have become more godlike, and therefore more loving, during the millenniums since he trod the Via Dolorosa. Assuredly he has not attained a stage whereunto Goethe might fitly have preceded him.

There is, however, no greater mistake, I imagine, than the fundamental one of supposing that any "self-losing," "absorption," or merging of personality of one kind or another, can possibly form a step of *progress* hereafter. The advance through inorganic, vegetative, animated, conscious, and self-conscious existence, and again from the lowest savage to the loftiest philosopher or heroic martyr, is all in the direction of a more and more perfect, complete, and definite personality. The severance of the Ego from the Non-ego may, indeed, be held in one sense to be the supreme result of all the machinery of the physical life; and the whole history of thought tends to show that a better recognition of the distinction has been at the root of the superiority of the Western over the Eastern and classic nations. Morality, of course, is grounded in it; and the ages before personality was clearly self-conscious were necessarily, like the years of infancy, ages before morality. To suppose that there is a height in the range of being, whereto having attained, this supreme, slowly-evolved personality suddenly collapses like a volcanic island, and subsides into the ocean of impersonal being, in which "He" becomes "It," is to suppose that the whole scheme of things is self-stultifying, a great "much ado about nothing," the building-up of a tower which should reach to heaven, but which is, in truth, only a child's house of cards, to be swept flat as soon as the coping is laid on it.

The meeting of two souls here or hereafter in perfect affection is not, as our inadequate and misleading metaphors often seem to imply, a blending in which personality is lost, but, rather, the act wherein personality comes out into most definite form. As in strong moral effort or vivid religious consciousness, so in the not less sacred outburst of pure human love, the intensity with which we admire, revere, sympathize with, embrace soul to soul the soul of a friend, is like the heat which brings out all the hidden scriptures on our hearts. We are never so truly ourselves as when we go out of ourselves. And as Emerson says that "the first requisite for friendship is to be able to do without friendship," so it is those natures which are most self-sustained, and possess the most vigorous and defined personality, with smallest of blurred and slovenly margins, which are most capable of vivid and stringent friendship. And, on the other hand, there are people who may rather be said to *slop over* into each other — to invade each other's personality, and lose their own — than to be united, as true friends ought to be, like the Rhone and the Arve, absolutely clear and distinct even when running side by side in the same channel.

IV. The moral condition of the dead is (as I have remarked) the one point concerning them on which the thought of Christendom has persistently fastened. Yet it has fixed on a view of that moral state which originated in a comparatively dark and rude age of ethical feeling, and must necessarily have given place long ago to higher conceptions, were it not for the stereotyping process by which the Cyclopædia of Religious Knowledge supposed to be contained in the two Testaments has been closed against either correction or amendment for eighteen centuries. While our clergy say as little as they can help about the eternity of torment, we are all aware that any serious attempt to remove the doctrine from the church formularies, or even to place the dogmas of the resurrection of the body, and the physical penalties with which it is threatened, in the category of open questions, would be met by invincible opposition. We have conquered from the adherents of the Book of Genesis the million ages of past geologic time; but the million millions of ages of future torment in the lake of fire we have by no means won from the disciples of the Book of the Apocalypse. They will give up almost any doctrine sooner than this. As Theodore Parker said, they cry out in dismay, when such a thing is named, "What? give up hell? our own eternal hell? Never, never, never!"

We shall accomplish very little, however, towards the removal of this dreadful cloud from the souls of men by merely pointing out how gloomy it is, or even by proving how it darkens the face of the Sun of righteousness. Consciously or unconsciously, it is felt by the orthodox to be a necessary part of their whole scheme of theology; and the atonement, which is their rainbow of hope, would fade and disappear, were that black cloud to pass away from behind it. Our only course is to do justice to the profound sentiment of the infinite solemnity of moral realities, the "exceeding sinfulness of sin," out of which sprung such ideas, and then, if possible, show how the same sentiment, guided by the calmer reflection and more refined ethical judgment of a later age, may project other ideas of a future world, vindicating the divine Justice and Love, no longer as in the awful diptych of an eternal heaven and an eternal hell, but in one harmonious picture of a world of souls all ascending by various paths, thorny or flower-strewn, towards the Father's throne. It cannot be doubted, I apprehend, that it was the intense sense of the horror and ill-desert of sin, which impressed itself on the minds of the first teachers of Christianity as the correlative of their new-born sense of the love of God, which drove them to make the future world of retribution darker, more hopeless, and embracing a larger class of souls, than any other prophets ever painted it. Christianity is nearly the only religion in the world which teaches that there is such a thing as eternal torture, and that it awaits ordinary sinners.

The paradox, that this should be the lesson of the creed which also teaches more clearly than any other that "God is love," is explicable only on the hypothesis, that with the fresh conviction of God's goodness came likewise to the early Christians a fresh conviction of the heinousness of human guilt. They could actually see no light through it at all. Christ himself never said a word implying that Dives would ever taste one cooling drop, that the "worm" would ever die, or the fire of hell ever be quenched. But, then, there is no token in the New Testament that he, or any of his apostles, dreamed of composing a scheme of theology such as Calvin and Jonathan Edwards delighted to construct; each doctrine dovetailing neatly into the next till the whole terrible "puzzle" is square and complete. Had they done so, it could hardly have been but that most merciful Heart which uttered such tender words of peace and pardon to Magdalen, and the adulteress, and the crucified thief, or even his who wrote the Epistles to Timothy and to Philemon, would have thrilled with horror at the thought that they were practically bequeathing to Christendom for eighteen centuries the idea of a God whose cruelty should exceed that of all the tyrants of Persia or of Rome, and towards whom men should lift their tear-worn eyes, divided ever between natural filial trust and the abject terror of slaves awaiting their doom. Viewed from the side of man, and man's guilt, they could threaten limitless punishment of sin. Had they looked at it from the side of God, and thought what the character of the Creator involved and guaranteed, it would have been, I venture to affirm, impossible for Christ or his followers to have left this hideous dogma of a world of perdition, unrelieved by the assurance, that, even into the lowest pit of sin and suffering, the Father's love should penetrate, and the Father's arm lift up the fallen.[1]

But if, on the one hand, human guilt must remain for us, as for the greatest souls of the past, an abyss of darkness we cannot fathom; and, on the other hand, the goodness of God stands out rounded into such an orb that we

[1] A MS. sermon by an old divine, Archbishop Cobbe, affirms that the Greek words in St. Matthew, signifying "Thou fool," were probably translated from the Aramaic original, and might be rendered more accurately, "Thou reprobate." I know not on what authority the archbishop made this statement; but, if verifiable, it would mark a very curious anomaly in the teaching of Christ. He condemned it as a mortal sin, deserving of hell-fire, for a *man* to treat his brother as irreclaimable and morally worthless. Yet he taught that the *Father* would actually consign that brother, as *such*, to eternal perdition.

know evermore, that "in him is no darkness at all," nor in his universe any final evil, — how are the two truths to be reconciled? How are we to avoid subtracting somewhat from our sense of the ill-desert of sin, while affirming with fearless confidence that it is finite and evanescent? I believe this is a problem having a very practical bearing on the religious life of the time; and I doubt very much whether the common substitute for the doctrine of the eternity of future physical pain — namely, a definite period of such pain after death — will at all meet the requirements of the case. Whatever be the relations of pain and sin (and I am far from denying that they exist), they are not of a kind which wholly satisfy the mind. They seem to offer a *form* of retribution, and a *method* of restoration, but not necessarily to constitute one or the other. Something different from mere suffering is needful to complete an "atonement" (or renewal of union) between the sinful soul and the divine Holiness. Not every "fire" would be a "purgatory." In fact, among the mysterious uses of pain, it is hardly possible to reckon it as a simple counterpoise thrown into the scale against guilt, and of itself adjusting the balance of justice. Those who hold that there is no such thing as punishment in the divine order, and those who hold that a certain definite modicum of pain apportioned to each sin fulfils that order, seem to me equally to err.

Surely the clew to the truth must lie in some other direction? Our bodies, with their pleasures and pains, are so much a part of ourselves now, that our moral lessons must necessarily come to us partly through them. Very naturally, that intimate union and its consequences were transferred in the imagination of the men of old to another world; and the doctrine of the resurrection of the flesh (which happened to descend to us with more valuable heirlooms in one line of our mental pedigree) has served to give some sort of color to our persistence in their ideas. But, looking at the matter from the standpoint of modern psychology, it is hard to see what we can have to do beyond the grave with physical pains of any kind. Of course, it is possible to imagine that the new bodies with which we may (or may not) be clothed should, from the first, be inlets of suffering. But as they can hardly be supposed to receive the taint of the diseases of the poor sin-stained frames left in the grave, whatever pains they may endure must be conceived of as purely arbitrary, and of a kind bearing no analogy to any order of the divine government with which we are acquainted.

But, though it is most difficult to conceive of *physical* suffering under the conditions of a new life (unless as the reflex of more sensitive frames with the sufferings of the soul), it is, on the contrary, almost saliently obvious, that the disembodied soul must immediately pass into a state wherein *mental* pain proportioned to its moral guilt will be unavoidable. We have no need to imagine a burning vault, pit of devils, or any other machinery of the divine inquisition: the mere fact of disembodiment, it would seem, must adequately account for all that is needed to work out the ends of justice.[1]

In those rare hours when the claims of the body are for a time partially suspended, — when we are neither hungry nor thirsty, nor somnolent nor restless; when no objects distract our eyes, and no sounds play upon the ear; when we feel, in a word, neither pain nor want nor

1 "When the portals of this world have been passed, when time and sense have been left behind, and this 'body of death' has dropped away from the liberated soul, every thing which clouded the perception, which dulled the vision, which drugged the conscience, while on earth, will be cleared off like the morning mist. *We shall see things as they really are*, ourselves and our sins among the number. No other punishment, whether retributive or purgatorial, is needed. Naked truth, unfilmed eyes, will do all that the most righteous vengeance could desire" (ENIGMAS, p. 260). The following two pages of this essay are among the most beautiful and striking in the range of literature.

pleasure, from our corporeal frames, — we obtain in a few moments more self-insight than in weeks and months of ordinary life. A prolongation of such a condition under disease, wherein (in some rare cases) the body's wants are reduced to a *minimum* without such positive pain as to occupy the mind, — in interminable, sleepless nights, and days when in solitude and silence the hours go by almost uninterrupted by those changes of sensation produced in healthy life by food, ablutions, and exercise, — then, it would seem (from the testimony of those who have passed through such experience), the soul becomes self-conscious to a degree quite inconceivable under ordinary conditions. The physical life falls comparatively into the background; the spiritual and moral life come forward; and the facts of our relations towards God, our sense of past transgressions, and our hopes of existence beyond the nearly-opened grave, become realities quite as sensibly felt as those of our bodily surroundings. We have but to imagine one degree more of such separation from physical interruptions and sensations, and conceive ourselves as actually severed from the body; and it becomes clear that we should instantly, and from that circumstance alone, pass into a purgatory. Even if we should retain no *recollection* of the special sins of earth, their *consequences* — sensible at iast in our degraded natures, our mean and malignant sentiments, our withered hearts — would be the heaviest curse. Every thing we have ever done of evil has undoubtedly left its stain on us in ways like these, even should the actual recollection of it be effaced with the brain-record of memory. *We* — our very selves, whatever in us can possibly survive the dissolution of the body — must carry with us, nay, rather *in* us, these dreadful results. As Theodore Parker says quaintly, " The saddler does not remember every stitch he took when a 'prentice; but every stitch served to make him a saddler." So every act we have done of good or evil, every sentiment we have indulged of loving or hateful, has gone to make us saints or sinners. We may repent the past, abhor it, renounce it, with the whole force of God-supported will; but, as even Aristotle knew, " of this even God is deprived, to make the past not to have been." The sins *have* been committed; and the trail of them over our souls must remain, even if we forget them one by one.

But if (as seems infinitely more consonant with the divine order) we pass through no river of oblivion on leaving the world, but, on the contrary, find all the past unrolling itself in one long unbroken panorama from the hour of death backward to the first hours of childish consciousness, then will our purgatory be complete indeed. Then, as we look, unhurried, dispassioned, at one hour of mortal life after another, remembering all we felt and did in it, all the weaknesses and mixed motives which spoiled our purest moments, all the selfishness, the bitterness, the ingratitude, perchance the sensual vice or cruel vindictiveness, which blackened the worst, then in very truth shall we learn at last — what it has been idly dreamed that only hell could teach — "the exceeding sinfulness of sin." The thought is almost too tremendous to dwell upon; yet it is but the simplest consequence from the laws of mind, as we know them. There is no need for the Almighty to bare his arm, and hurl us into the lake of fire. He has only to leave us alone with our sins, to draw the curtain between us and the world, and our punishment must come with unerring certainty.

This is the awful purgatory which I believe awaits us all. Is there nothing but terror in it for the sinner, and sadness for the saint? Nay, but is there not, also, somewhat of deep and stern satisfaction? At the best moments of life, have we not longed for such an insight into our own dark souls, such a sense of the guilt which we dimly knew existed, but under which our hardened consciences remained numb? Will it not be something gained, when the scales which ever cover our eyes when we strive to look inward shall fall from them at last? We shall then know, and be *sure* we know truly, what is the whole evil of our hearts, the sinfulness of our acts. There will be no more uncertainty, and fear of self-delusion, of walking in a vain shadow of self-acquittal, or, it may be, of ill-allotted self-condemnation. We shall know our true place in the moral world, our true relation to the all-holy God. And we shall not only know what is true, but suffer what is just. We shall endure all the agony, and also learn the infinite relief, of a repentance at last adequate, and proportioned to our sinfulness. The pain will fall, where it ought to fall, upon our hearts themselves; and as Cranmer held his "guilty hand" to the fire, so, perchance, shall we, instead of striving to escape, even desire to hold them to their torture. That entire, absolute, perfect repentance will be the great and true expiation; and, when it has been accomplished, the blessed justice of God will be vindicated, and all will be well.

Is there an outlook beyond this purgatory, wherein time can have no meaning? Assuredly there must be. There yet must remain for the souls which God has made and purified both work to do for him, and joy in him and in one another. There must be the service of his creatures, the learning of his truth, the reconciliation with every foe, the re-union of immortal affection, and the everlasting approach, nearer and nearer through the infinite ages, to perfect goodness, and to Him who is supremely good. But these things lie afar off, where eye hath not seen, nor ear heard, nor the heart of man conceived, the things which God hath prepared for those who love him, ay, and for those, also, who now love him not.

DOOMED TO BE SAVED.

DOOMED TO BE SAVED.

IN old times, two or three centuries ago, men believed that they could sell their souls to the Devil. No one seems to think such a bargain possible now, though the belief in the existence of the strange Incarnate Evil, the Great Bad God, with whom it was supposed to be transacted, still forms part of the accepted creed of Christendom. I am not concerned now to discuss the absurdity and blasphemy involved in this doctrine of a cruel and relentless Wolf left freely by the Shepherd of souls to prowl forever through his hapless fold. But I shall ask of you to dwell in imagination, for a few moments, on the state of one of the hundreds of men and women who formerly believed with unhesitating credulity that they had bartered their existence to the Fiend, and were henceforth forevermore, and without hope of escape, the sworn servants of Satan.

Probably such imaginary transactions generally happened somewhat in this way. A man was violently goaded by vindictiveness to desire the ruin of an enemy, or by want or avarice to long for gold, or by passionate love to covet the possession of the person he loved. At the same time he entertained, undoubtingly, the dangerous belief that there was a power always at hand ready to gratify his desires at the price of a penalty to be paid only in the distant future. If we attempt to realize the terrible, ever-present temptation which such a belief would offer, I think it will appear only too natural, that, in some moment when his longings were most vehement, the tempted wretch should say, "*I will* be revenged," or "*I will* be rich," or "*I will* gain the woman I love, even if I lose my soul! I will give myself to the Devil forever, if he will do for me what I want." Supposing, after this, by some perfectly natural chance, the man did obtain his end, his enemy fell sick or died, a little money unexpectedly came in his way, or the woman he loved returned his passion, from that moment, he would inevitably conclude Satan had accepted the bargain, and fulfilled his part of the contract. There was no more retrocession possible. He was no more free to draw back, and give up his coveted gains. Hell had hold of him by a bond which could never be broken. He was the servant of sin, outlawed from God and heaven, and the society of the good and innocent, and destined, without hope of pardon or reprieve, to pass, whenever his new master chose to call him, to the realms of everlasting torture and despair. What, I ask, would be the result on a man's character of finding himself so doomed? I think, that, after the first flush of gratified passion had subsided, the poor deluded wretch must always have felt creeping over him a horror such as no experience of our lives can render altogether comprehensible. Even the fact of his success (being at the same time the pledge that the barter was actually made) must have brought with it a thrill of unspeakable awe. Then as time went on, and the gratified desire sank down among his passions, while natural affections and harmless interests resumed their ordinary sway, there would begin a period of unmitigated agony. No innocent pursuit could be followed, no pure affection cherished, no kindly action performed; for the man would know that he would be an object of loathing and horror to the nearest and dearest, did they understand his real condition, and that none would take a gift from his hand. Every allusion made by those around him to religion, the memory of his own innocent childhood, the spectacle of death and interment, would each be like a fresh lash of despair. By degrees, I believe, even a very bad and irreligious man, finding thus every avenue to good closed to him, would begin to envy every beggar by the wayside, every dying sufferer in the hospital, nay, every criminal going to the gallows, who was not, like himself, utterly and eternally shut out from God and goodness. Of course, the belief in the futility and hopelessness of any repentance on his part, the idea that the Fiend would laugh, were he to attempt to pray, would finally drive him into absolute recklessness and hardness of heart. He would say, "Evil, be thou my good," and give himself up to such gross pleasures, such malignity, cruelty, perfidy, and blasphemy, as his miserable heart might choose in its despair. Looking back after the lapse of ages to the historical proofs that our fellow-men have actually gone through this hideous torture, we feel now as if the nightmare must have been more than the brain of man could bear, and that the having caused such direful woe must be added to the long list of terrors, persecutions, and ascetisms, which go farther, perhaps, than Christians commonly imagine, to counterbalance the benefits which humanity has received from their creed. If the faith which had its origin in the pure spirit of Christ, but which so soon became corrupted, has indeed bound up many a broken heart, it has also assuredly broken many,—in monasteries and nunneries, in the dungeons of the Inquisition, ay, and in Protestant homes, whence guiltless and believing souls have been driven into mad-houses, under the terrors of the unpardonable sin.

But for us, who neither believe it possible to sell our souls at all, nor in a Devil to whom we might sell them, is there any lesson in this sad old story? I think there must be one; for we believe *exactly the reverse* of that hideous doctrine which drove these poor wretches to destruction. Our faith teaches us that our only Lord is goodness itself impersonated; and that we are not "sold" to him by any act of our own, not even "reconciled" to him by any atonement or mediator, but are his by birthright and by nature,— his as the child belongs to its parent,— his as a man's thought is his own. We are each of us thoughts of God. We owe our being to *having been* in that infinite Mind; and, as the author of the Book of Wisdom says, "Never wouldst thou have made any thing, hadst thou not loved it." The Creator cannot disgusted be with his creature's infirmities, or wearied of his weakness, or ready to abandon him because of his sin ; for he has understood it all from the first ; and in his book were all our transgressions written, when as yet there were none of them, and we hung as innocent babes upon our mothers' breasts.

I know that this faith is held by us in the very teeth of scores of passages in the Bible, and of the denunciation of ten thousand orthodox divines. Nay, there are some even among those who have left orthodoxy far behind, who yet hold that it is both a false, and especially a dangerous, creed to teach men that God loves them always, and that they are certain to be saved (to use the much misapplied old phrase) at last. Let us inquire more carefully how this may be, seeing that, in a great measure, the practical side of our religion depends on our sense of the matter.

I think it will be found that sin looks very differently in proportion as we regard it from its own level, or from a little higher up, or from a region still farther above it. The man who is quite on a level with the sin, who is himself cruel, unchaste, deceitful, dishonest, drunken, hears always of another falling into his sin with a certain evil pleasure. As we say, it "keeps him in countenance," and prevents him feeling shame. He finds no jests so diverting as those which tell of cheats and drunken brawls, adulteries and filth. A large mass of literature, from the old story of Gil Blas and Fielding's novels, down to the latest French romances, prove how widespread is this taste for tales of vice, this propensity to "rejoice in iniquity."

But when a man has begun in earnest to try and amend his own life, and has learned to hate his own sins, he ceases to find any thing amusing or ridiculous in the sins of others. His feeling about them becomes one of righteous anger, if the offence involve cruelty or perfidy; of disgust and loathing, if it be one of sensual vice. He wishes heartily that justice may be done on the offender; and, beyond this, he has no feeling towards him but contempt and abhorrence. Fortunately the majority of people in every civilized community have attained at least so far as this point; and it is, so far as it goes, a very sound standing-ground, and one infinitely superior either to the pleasure of the grossly wicked, or to the sentimental softness and laxity about crime, which is one of the evil fashions of our day. I confess, when I hear of a mob being with difficulty prevented from tearing to pieces some monster who has committed an act of dastardly cruelty, I cannot altogether regret the exhibition of righteous popular indignation; and, on the other hand, I know few worse symptoms of national moral health than a great crowd cheering and doing honor to a villain.

But does no man, I would ask, get beyond the stage of mere anger at crime? I think even very poor aspirants after goodness do so, especially if they are parents. Suppose a man or a woman to have striven for years to bring up a young lad in honesty and religion; to have watched his boyish faults and repentances, his efforts to do well, and his sorrow and shame when he failed. At the end of all, the elder friend hears, perhaps, that the youth has committed a forgery, or seduced an innocent girl, or has sunk into habits of perpetual drunkenness. What are the feelings with which he receives the sad tidings? Surely they are very different from mere anger and indignation, and a fierce desire to punish the offender? He will, indeed, feel (inasmuch as he is human) a horrible shock of surprise and disappointment, and also, perhaps, some personal resentment, that all his good counsels have been thrown away. But beyond all this, and far more deeply, he will grieve that such wickedness should be done, and done by the man he knows so well, whose soul has so often lain bare to him, who was capable of so much better things. He will understand how certain faults in his nature, certain temptations in his lot, have led him on, step by step, till he has been entangled in sin, and has fallen so miserably. And then his heart will go out in pity and compassion unutterable towards the unhappy one. He will know that his condition is infinitely deplorable, — that if he repent, and feel his guilt, he must endure agonies of remorse; and that if he be callous, and feel it not, it is so much the worse. He will estimate the man's misfortunes as ten thousand times heavier than if he had lost his health or wealth, or become blind or maimed. And if he be the father or master of the offender, and obliged in some way to visit his transgression with punishment, he will earnestly strive, that, even in punishing him, he may do him good, and bring him to a better mind, so as to lead to his restoration to peace and virtue, and entire reconciliation with himself.

Now, I challenge those who forbid us to believe in the infinite mercy of God to say which of these three ways of viewing sin is most godlike, most probably nearest to the way in which God must view it. Will he feel *pleasure* in it? Assuredly not. Will he feel mere *anger* and wrathful indignation? I think it was very natural that the old Hebrews, who had just reached that stage themselves, should suppose he did so; but I also think that it is monstrous for a race who have for two thousand years taken Christ's blessed parable of the Prodigal Son as the very word of God to do any thing of the kind. I think, if we were not caught in the meshes of that wretched Augustinian scheme of theology, which makes the atonement necessary to appease God's wrath, and postulates eternal hell to compel us to accept it, — I think, I say, if it were not for this theology, all Christendom must have long ago come to see, that, at the very least, God feels towards a sinner as a father or a saint would do, and not as a man less good or wise or merciful, — the great *Policeman* of the universe. And remember, when we are presuming to speak of the awful character of God, it is not our business to inquire what it is *just possible* he may be or do without injustice or cruelty, but what is the very highest, the noblest, the kindest, the most royal and fatherlike, thing we can possibly lift our minds to conceive. When we have found *that*, we may be assured it is the nearest we can yet approach to the truth. By and by, when we are loftier, nobler, and kinder, too, we shall get nearer to it still. Of all impossible things, the most impossible must surely be, that a *man* should dream something of the good and the noble, and that it should prove, at last, that his Creator was less good and less noble than he had dreamed. We theists, then, I conceive, are justified (even in this dim world of imperfect and uncertain vision) in holding clearly and boldly, as the very core of our faith, that God loves eternally and unalterably every creature he has made; and that our sin, while it draws a thick veil over our eyes, and makes it impossible to give us the joy of communion with him, yet never changes him, never blackens that Sun of love in the heavens.

Nor is it only by argument and analogy that we come to this conclusion. The Lord of conscience, who bids *us* forgive till seventy times seven; the Lord of life, the Father of spirits, who reveals himself to us in the supreme hour of heartfelt prayer; that God whose voice has so often called us back from our wanderings, and put it into our hearts to pray, and then has blessed and restored us again and yet again, — that God, we know, is never to be alienated.

He is our Guide for ever and ever, Friend, Master, Father, Lord. As physically we live and move and have our being in him, so morally we live in his bosom, and are surrounded by his love and pity. Poor, froward, rebellious babes, struggling now with the pains of mortality, and now stretching out vain hands of longing to seize forbidden joys,—with all our wrestlings and struggles we never fall out of his arms. They close round us, even at our worst. The Calvinists hold, as one of their "Five Points," the "Final Perseverance of the Saints." We theists believe in that "perseverance" too, and are persuaded that no human heart which has once known the unutterable bliss of loving God can ever forget it, or cease to yearn to return from every wandering to his feet. But we also believe in the final salvation of those who are *not* saints, but sinners, nay, of the very worst and most hardened of mankind. As one of the wisest men I ever knew (the late Matthew Davenport Hill) once said to me, "I believe in the *aggressive* power of love and kindness, and in the comparative weakness of every obstacle of evil or stubbornness which can be opposed thereto." We do not think man's evil can, in the long-run of the infinite ages, outspeed finally God's ever-pursuing mercy. He *must* overtake us sooner or later. True, it may be late, very late, before he does so; not necessarily in this world, not, perchance, in the next world to come. We may doom ourselves to groan beneath the burden of sin, and writhe beneath the scourge of just and most merciful retribution, again and yet again, no one knows how long. We may choose evil rather than good, and vileness instead of nobleness, and be ungrateful and sinful almost as he is long-suffering and infinitely holy; but it is *almost*, not *quite*. God will get the better of us at last.

Is this indeed a "dangerous creed"? Will men be the worse and harder, and more daringly wicked, for holding it? My friends, we are all, I fear, very unworthy types of what theists should be; nay, I have never yet seen man or woman, not that hero-soul Theodore Parker, not that true saint of God, Keshub Chunder Sen, who altogether and perfectly attained those alpine heights to which theism should lift us. But yet even at our weakest, we know that we are not the worse for believing in the infinite goodness of God. Was any one ever the worse for having an earthly father who would grieve, or a mother who would weep and pray for him in his sin, rather than curse him, and cast him off? Human nature is bad enough: I am not disposed to underrate its vices and meanness. But with all my soul I repudiate and reject the blasphemy that it can grow worse for having a better knowledge of God.

The results of a settled faith that we are inevitably destined to become good and blessed ought obviously to be as nearly as possible the precise converse of the results of the belief of the poor wretch who imagined he had sold himself to the Power of Evil. Just as he must have looked round, and envied the meanest or most suffering of mankind, so we must look upon the happiest or most fortunate who hold darker creeds as far less blessed than ourselves. To *them*, half the horizon is covered by a great lurid cloud, out of which come the thunders and the bolts of doom, and which may at any moment blot out the sun forever from their sight, even as they believe that to tens of thousands of the dead he is hid forevermore. For *us*, that shroud of blackness has rolled utterly away; and the glory of God shines wide as earth and heaven, showering blessings on the head of every creature he has made. It is only our own dim eyes, blinded by the mists of sin and selfishness, which sometimes fail to see him.

And again: just as the Fiend-bought man

dreamed it was of no use for him to try to return to virtue, or to yield to the softening of his heart when the sweet dews of penitence fell on him (as they fall sometimes on us all): so we, on the contrary, must needs know that it is *no use* for us to persist in rebellion, and harden ourselves against the thought of God's love. We are *doomed* (O blessed doom!) to be conquered at last, and brought in remorse and shame, and yet with the infinite peace of restoration, to our Father's arms. We are *destined* to be noble, not base; pure, not unholy; loving, not selfish or malicious. Sooner or later throughout the cycles of our immortality, all the vile sensuality, the yet more hideous hate and malice which we sometimes hug now to our hearts, must fall off us like loathsome, outworn rags, and be trampled under our feet with disgust and shame. We never sink our souls in gross and unholy pleasures now, but we are befouling them with mire which hereafter we shall wash away with rivers of tears. We never utter a cruel or slanderous word, or hurt a child or a brute, but we are making a wound in our hearts which will smart long, long, after our victim has forgotten its pain. Nay, we never miss an opportunity of giving innocent pleasure, or of helping another soul on the path to God, but we are taking away from ourselves forever what might have been a happy memory, and leaving in its place a remorse. A French cynic (who could not have known what friendship meant) advises us to "live with our friends as if they might one day become our enemies." A good Englishman reversed the maxim, and bade us "live with our enemies as if they might one day become our friends." My fellow-theists, it is not for us a matter of chance that our enemies *may* one day become our friends, but of firm faith that they *will* one day do so; that, as Mahomet said, "the blessed shall sit beside one another, and all grudges shall be taken away out of their hearts." Why, even the approach of holy death heals our miserable quarrels now, and softens our bitterest animosity. When we have crossed the dark river, and climbed but a little way towards the city of God beyond, every thing resembling hatred and jealousy and malice and spite will have died out of our souls. Only where their baleful fires have burned, there must long remain a black spot charred and blistering.

And as to God: when we come a little more to know him, a little to understand what love he bears us, how he fulfils all our dreams of what the highest, the most lovable, and adorable can be, that which our own hearts from their depths spontaneously love and adore,—when, I say, we come to know somewhat more of all this, how shall we look back on our hardness and our ingratitude? The tears of an unworthy son upon a mother's grave must be less bitter than ours. God will forgive us; but when shall we be able to forgive ourselves?

These are, in our faith, the certainties of the future. We are *sure* that we must repent every sin, and rise out of every weakness, till we become, at last, meet to be called the sons and daughters of the Lord Almighty. Assuredly the conviction that such things are in store should not leave us passive now, any more than it could be indifferent to the man who had sold himself to the Fiend that he was irrevocably destined to perdition. At the bottom of our hearts, I think, there is, even at our worst and weakest, a wish to be good, a dumb longing to be brave, upright, truthful, sober, deserving of our own esteem. Perhaps our ideal is not very high; we do not hunger and thirst after any very exalted and self-denying righteousness; but, at least, we wish we were better than we are. The German poet Schiller says, that no man ever loves evil for evil's sake, as he may love good for goodness' sake. He only chooses evil, because, contingently, it includes what is agreeable, or saves what is disagreeable. This is the lowest platform on which, I believe, we ever stand permanently, though now and then some of us may be able to understand all too well what the wretch did whom we have been considering, who gave himself up to the powers of darkness, or, as St. Paul says, determined to "work all iniquity with greediness." There are some of us who can look back to such black eclipses of all the better life in us, when deliberately, and with our eyes open, we resolved to do some wicked thing, even though we saw beyond it a long vista of other sins and deceits, and practically in doing it threw our whole future into the balance of evil. Looking back to such days (if any such there be in our memory), we tremble as in remembering how once, perchance, we hung helpless over a terrific precipice, till some strong hand lifted us up; or how we were sinking in the waters of a fathomless sea, when some plank was thrown to us, to which we clung, and were saved. Again: there are some of us who have risen a little above either of these states, who have long turned their backs on the dreadful temptations of a life of resolute sin and self-indulgence, and who do a little more than vaguely wish to be better, or pray (as St. Augustine says he did in his youth), "Make me holy, *but not yet.*" They desire to be holy *now* and at once. They have learned to hate and loathe their remaining faults, "the sin which doth so easily beset them," and to wish, beyond all earthly wishes, for strength

"To feel, to think, to do,
Only the holy right,
To yield no step in the awful race,
No blow in the fearful fight;"

to be "perfect even as their Father which is in heaven is perfect."

But whether our desire to be good and noble be only a feeble and faint aspiration, dimly felt amid the tumult of life's toil and passion, or the supreme and conscious longing of our souls, — in either case, I think the faith that we are *made for* such goodness is calculated (if we could but realize it aright) to carry with it an immeasurable power to strengthen us, to fan our little spark of holy ambition into a flame which might burn on God's own altar. The Parsees, the disciples of Zoroaster, have, among their prayers in the Zendavesta, the direction that every believer should say every morning, as he fastens his girdle, "Douzakh (hell) will be destroyed at the resurrection; and Ormuzd (the Lord of good) shall reign over all forever." Not amiss, I think, was their ritual devised, to make the first thought of each opening day one of moral encouragement, and of hope assured in the final victory of light over darkness, virtue over vice, and joy over sorrow and pain. I do not say that good men have not been ready to lead a forlorn hope, and fight the good fight, even in a world they believed doomed to perdition, with the terror before their eyes, that even they themselves might become, as St. Paul said of himself, perhaps "a castaway." But, beyond all doubt, it is a very different thing to wage that awful and relentless war with inward and outward evil, if we can but see, like Constantine's Conquering Legion, far away in the heavens the signals of victory. To look round on our fellow-men, the worst and weakest, — or, what is far harder to understand, the *basest*, — and believe with firm assurance, that they are one day to be worthy of all the love and honor we can give them, — this is to enable us to love and labor for them now, and to have patience, as God has patience, with the weight of clay which overlays so heavily their little seed of good. And still more, to look into our own souls, and trust that one day we shall be pure, one day all the vileness there shall be burnt out, one day we shall live in that upper air of noble feelings and high thoughts, into which, now and then, we have just risen in some hour of prayer, to sink again in shameful failure to the dust,—to trust that all *this* is in store for us, is to lift us up out of the slough of our despond, and renew our strength like the eagle's. I suppose there are not many of us who have advanced many steps along that brief way which leads from the cradle to the grave, without having sad reason to feel weary and disgusted with themselves, and their futile efforts to amend. As the old hymn of Charles Wesley says they have cried a hundred times, "This only once forgive," and then they have sinned again, till at last the power of feeling any thing like acute repentance has passed away, and they have ceased to hope very much that they will ever grow better in this world. There is nothing in all life so sad as this November of the soul. The scorching suns of summer passion, the April showers of youthful remorse, would be infinitely better than this colorless, dim, moral life, so chill, so unhopeful. But, even for this, the faith in the eternal love of God is the return of spring. Brothers and sisters, if you have felt this deadness fall on you, remember that it has no place, no reason, in our creed. We may be cold and dull and unrepenting; we may know even the horrible experience that we have greatly failed, greatly sinned, and yet have no tear of anguish, no heartfelt throb of remorse, to give to our shameful past: yet this is all *our* misery, and deadness of heart, not *God's* withdrawal. We cannot help ourselves. But our Father in heaven, he who desires our righteousness more than we ever desire it, whose "will is our salvation," — *he* can help us, he *will* help us. We have learned our own weakness: now is the time to learn his almighty strength. It is not for us to despair of growing, not merely pure, but good, not merely good, but holy. God has made us for that very thing; and what God intends, *that* assuredly will at last be done. He is not wearied of us: it is we who are weary of our vain and vacillating selves. I cannot use the accustomed phrase, that "he will forgive us if we pray." He is *always* forgiving. He stands by every hour, watching all our poor struggles, with pity and love ineffable, longing — yes! I believe we may dare to say it — longing for our return, that he may bless us once more with the consciousness of his love, the sense of re-union with his holiness, the infinite, immeasurable, awful joy of giving ourselves to be his in soul and body on earth, — his to do his holy will in worlds beyond the grave, forever and forever.

Father, blessed Father! Take us thus back! From all our wanderings, our coldness, our miserable guilt and rebellion, our baseness and our sin, redeem us, O God! Father, we love thee, — only a little now; but we shall love thee hereafter wholly and perfectly. Take our hearts, and mould them to thyself. We give them to thee. That which thou desirest for us, even the same do we desire. Fulfil thy blessed purposes in us. As thou hast made us to be pure and good, so burn thou out of our souls all our sinfulness. As thou hast made us to be strong and holy, so do thou strengthen us with might by thy Spirit in the inner man. Show us all the depth of the evil, the sensuality, the bitterness of heart, the coldness towards thee in which we have lived, and the glory and beauty and blessing of the life of love to thee and to our fellows, which it is in our power yet to live. Lift us out of the pit, out of the mire and clay, and set our feet upon a rock, and order all our goings. We are thine, O Father and Mother of the world! we are thine — save us! We know that thou *wilt* save!

THE EVOLUTION OF THE SOCIAL SENTIMENT;

OR,

HETEROPATHY, AVERSION, AND SYMPATHY.

THE EVOLUTION OF THE SOCIAL SENTIMENT.

THERE is, perhaps, no human emotion which may not be described as infectious or epidemic, quite as justly as idiopathic or endemic. We "catch" cheerfulness or depression, courage or terror, love or hatred, cruelty or pity, from a gay or a mournful, a brave or a cowardly, an affectionate or malicious, a brutal or tender-hearted associate, fully as often as such feelings are generated in our own souls by the incidents of our personal experience. In the case of individuals of cold and weak temperaments, it may even be doubted whether they would ever hate, were not the poisoned shafts of an enemy's looks to convey the venom to their veins; nor love, did not the kiss of a lover kindle the unlighted fuel in their hearts. The sight of heroic daring stirs the blood of the poltroon to bravery, and the sound of a single scream of alarm conveys to whole armies the contagion of panic fear. Among the horrors of sieges and revolutions, the worst atrocities are usually committed by men and women, hitherto harmless, who suddenly exhibit the tiger passions of assassins and *petroleuses*, maddened with the infection of cruelty and slaughter. Sympathy, then, is not, properly speaking, one *kind* of emotion, but a spring in human nature whence every emotion may, in turn, be drawn, like the manifold liquids from a conjurer's bottle. In the following pages I shall, however, endeavor to trace its development only in the limited sense of that emotion to which we commonly give the name of sympathy *par excellence;* namely, the sentiment of pain which we experience on witnessing the pain of another person, and of pleasure in his pleasure, irrespective of any anticipated results, present or future, touching our personal interests. It has been hitherto assumed universally (so far as I am aware) that this precise emotion of sympathetic pain and pleasure has been felt in all ages by mankind; and that, allowance being made for warmer and colder temperaments, and for the intervention of stronger or weaker moral re-enforcements, we might take it for granted that every man, woman, and child, savage and civilized, has always felt, and will always feel, reflected pain in pain, and pleasure in pleasure.[1] It is the aim of the present paper to urge certain reasons for reconsidering this popular opinion, and for treating the emotion of sympathy as a sentiment having a natural history, and being normally progressive through various and very diverse phases; differing in all men, not solely according to their temperaments or moral self-control, but, still more emphatically, according to the stage of genuine civilization which they may have attained. It is superfluous to remark that this inquiry is an important one, and must, if successfully conducted, serve to throw no small light on the whole subject of the social affections. Here, in the electric commotion caused by the actual spectacle of vivid pain or pleasure, we must needs find the best marked among all the multifarious psychological phenomena which result from the

[1] Mr. Bain says (The Emotions and the Will, p. 113) that compassion has been manifested in every age of the world, and that "never has the destitute been utterly forsaken." Also (p. 210) that "the foundations of sympathy and imitation are the same;" and that, though "the power of *interpreting* emotional expression is acquired," some of the manifestations of feeling do *instinctively* excite the same kind of emotion in others, the principal instances occurring under the tender emotion. The moistened eye, and the sob, wail, or whine of grief, by a pre-established connection or coincidence, are at once signs and exciting causes of the same feeling."

collision of human souls. All our benevolence is, in truth, only the extension of such instant and vehement sympathy with actually witnessed pain or pleasure, into the remoter and less ascertained conditions of our fellow-creatures' sufferings and enjoyments: all our cruelty is only the perpetuation and exacerbation of the converse sentiment. As a flash of lightning is to latent electricity, such is the rapid and vivid emotion struck out in us by the sight of another's agony or ecstasy, compared with our calm, habitual social sentiments. Hitherto, little attention has been paid to such emotions, because (as above remarked) it has been assumed that they exhibit uniform phenomena; and that if a man be so far elevated above a senseless clod as to feel *any thing* at the sight of another's pain, that which he feels is always sympathetic pain; and, if he feel any thing at sight of pleasure, it is pleasure. So deeply, indeed, is this delusion rooted in our minds, that it is almost impossible, at the first effort, to dissever the idea of such sympathy from our conception of human nature in its rudest stage, much more to divide it from the sentiment of love, or avoid confounding the lack of it with personal hatred. With those whom we love (it is taken for granted) we must sympathize intensely, and with the rest of mankind in lesser measure, unless some special bar of antipathy intervene. But a little reflection will show that this is far from holding good as universally true. There is such a thing as love which is wholly a love of complacency, without admixture of benevolence; which seeks its own gratification, and is perfectly callous to the pains and joys of its object. And there is often absolute absence of sympathy between man and man, when no personal hatred exists to interfere with its expansion. The explanation of the facts must be found, if at all, by disentangling the roots of egotism and altruism (now so closely interwoven, but in their origin so far apart) at the very *nexus* of immediate sympathy, where one human heart reflects back in vivid emotion the emotion of another.

The first question which concerns us is: Does the description of sympathy, as above given, as the common sentiment of men and women at our stage of civilization, apply properly to the spontaneous sentiments of children and savages? Does their emotion at the sight of pain or pleasure take the same form as ours? and does it prompt them to similar actions? There are grounds, I believe, for denying that it does any thing of the kind, and for surmising that the emotion felt at such stages, at the sight of pain, is more nearly allied to anger and irritation than to tenderness and pity, and the emotion felt at the sight of pleasure, more akin to displeasure than to reflected enjoyment.

Before endeavoring to interpret the sentiments of savages in these matters, we shall do well to cast a preliminary glance at the behavior of the lower animals, concerning which we know somewhat more, and are less liable to be misled. Without assuming that the feelings of brutes supply, in a general way, any direct evidence regarding those of even the most degraded tribes of men, they may justly be held to afford useful indication of them in the case of those actions wherein brute and savage obviously coincide, while the sentiments of civilized humanity fail to supply any explation.

Of all the facts of natural history, none is better ascertained than the painful one that almost all kinds of animals have a propensity to destroy their sick and aged or wounded companions. The hound which has fallen off his bench, the wolf caught in a trap, the superannuated rook or robin, in truth, nearly all known creatures, wild or domesticated, undergo involuntary "euthanasia" from the teeth, bills, or claws of their hitherto friendly associates. It may be said to be the law of creation, that such destruction of the sick and aged should take place, — a law whose general beneficence, as curtailing the slow torments of hunger and decay, has properly been adduced by natural theologians to console us for its seeming repulsiveness and severity. The sight of another animal of its kind in agony appears to act on the brute as an incentive to destructive rage. He is vehemently excited, rushes at the sufferer, bellowing, barking, or screeching wildly, and commonly gores, bites, or pecks it till it dies. The decay of its aged companion, though it affects the animal less violently than its agony, stirs, somehow, the same instinct, which is the precise converse of helpful pity; and, if the species be gregarious, a whole flock or herd will often join to extinguish the last spark of expiring life in one of their own band. There are, of course, exceptions to this rule, especially among domesticated animals, which sometimes acquire gentler habits, and at one stage of advance merely forsake their sick companions, and at another actually help and befriend them. The broad fact, however, on which I desire to insist at this moment, is, that, at the sight of pain, animals generally feel an impulse to destroy rather than to help,—a passion more nearly resembling anger than tenderness. This emotion (to avoid continual circumlocution) will be indicated in the following pages by the term which seems most nearly to describe its chief characteristic; namely, *heteropathy.* It is the converse of "sympathy," as we understand that feeling; and it differs from "antipathy" as anger differs from hatred; heteropathy being the sudden and (possibly) transient emotion, and antipathy implying permanent dislike, with a certain combination of disgust.

The sight of the pleasure of another animal does not seem generally to convey more pleasure to the brute than the sight of another's pain inspires it with pity. As a rule, the beast displays, under such circumstances, emotions ludicrously resembling the exhibitions of human envy, jealousy, and dudgeon. Only will the friendly dog testify delight at his comrade's release from his chain, or the generous horse display satisfaction when his yoke-mate is turned out in the same field with him to graze.

Keeping these facts of animal life in view, we are surely justified in interpreting the murderous practices in vogue, to the present day, among many savage tribes (and formerly common all over the world) as *monumental institutions*, preserving still the evidence of the early sway of the same passion of heteropathy in the human race in its lowest stage of development. The half-brutal Fuegian, who kills and eats his infirm old grandfather, differs in no perceptible way, as regards his action, from the young robin which cruelly pecks to death the robin two generations older than himself. An equally widespread and similar impulse may fairly be assumed to account for actions so nearly identical in barbarian and in bird. The only appreciable difference is, that, as regards the savage, it would seem that custom (which must have originally sprung out of an instinct, or, at least, have been in harmony with it) has so long been stereotyped, that the act of human parricide is generally performed with unruffled calmness of demeanor, and even with some display of tenderness towards the father or mother, who is buried alive in Polynesia as kindly as he or she would have been put to bed by an affectionate son or daughter in England.[1]

[1] Sir J. Lubbock (Origin of Civilization, p. 248) quotes from Fiji and the Fijians an instance in which Mr. Hunt was invited by a young man to attend his mother's funeral. Mr. Hunt joined the procession, and was surprised to see no corpse; when the young man pointed out his mother, who was walking along with them as gay and lively, and apparently as much pleased, as anybody present. To Mr. Hunt's remonstrance, the young man only replied, that "she was

The same dispassionateness in the performance of the dreadful act seems, indeed, to have prevailed so far back as historical records extend, and we cannot (as it were) actually catch the brutal heteropathy in the fact of murder. Herodotus says the Masagetæ used in his time to kill, boil, and eat their superannuated relations, holding such to be the happiest kind of death.[1] Ælian describes the Sardinians as killing their fathers with clubs as an honorable release from the distresses of age. The Wends, even after the introduction of Christianity, are accused of cannibal practices of the like kind; and (Mr. Tylor adds) there still existed in Sweden, in many churches, so late as 1600, certain ancient clubs, "known as *ätta-klubbor*, or family-clubs, wherewith, in old days, the aged and hopelessly sick were solemnly killed by their kinsfolk."

their mother, and her sons ought to put her to death, now she had lived long enough." Eventually the old woman was ceremoniously strangled.

[1] See an article on Primitive Society, by E. Tylor: Contemporary Review, April, 1873. Mr. Tylor traces the custom to the necessities of wandering tribes, and says, that, after there is no longer the excuse of necessity, the practice may still go on, partly from the humane intent of putting an end to lingering misery, but perhaps more through the survival of a custom inherited from harder and ruder times. Necessity may explain desertion, but surely hardly murder and cannibalism.

Nevertheless, taking into consideration the law pervading the brute creation, and (as we shall presently see) the yet perceptible destructive impulse in the children of civilized regions, there seems to be ground for attributing the remote origin of all such practices, however tenderly performed within historic times, to the fierce instinct of the earliest savage, whom the sight of pain and helplessness excited just as it excites the bird or beast. In the wild animal, it still acts simply and unimpaired: in the man, even in his lowest present condition, it has been stereotyped into a custom.

Nor is it by any means only in the case of aged parents, that the heteropathy of the savage betrays itself. No similar custom of deliberate murder of the infirm has had room to grow up in the case of wives, who are, of course, usually younger than their husbands; and we do not therefore hear of a regular system of strangling them, when permanently diseased or incapacitated. They are only starved, beaten, and overtaxed with toil, till they expire in the way, unhappily, not unfamiliarly known to English coroners' juries as "Death from natural causes, accelerated by want of food, and harsh treatment." But, if heteropathy acts only indirectly on sickly wives, it exhibits itself in full force on puling and superfluous infants. Custom among numberless savages, and even among nations so far advanced in civilization as the ancient Greeks and modern Chinese, has regularly established child-murder precisely in those cases *in which the helplessness threatens to prove permanent*, and which, consequently, leave the destructive sentiment full play, though they would call forth the most passionate instincts of pity and protection among ourselves. A puny and deformed boy is, in the ruder state of society, an unendurable object to his parents, who, without troubling themselves about Spartan principles concerning the general interests of the community, silence his pitiful baby-wails at once and forever. Needless to add, no mercy can be expected for a daughter born where women are (to use Mr. Greg's phrase) "redundant." She is exposed or drowned, with less pity than a humane Englishman feels for a fly in his milk-jug.[1]

[1] See the Marquis de Beauvoir's hideous account of an evening walk outside the walls of Canton, with scores of dead and dying infants lying beside the path. A recent official Chinese Ukase on the subject of infanticide, translated in the correspondence of the Times, sufficiently corroborates these statements, and shows also, happily, some desire on the part of the government to put a stop to the practice. It is issued by the provincial treasurer of Hupei, who begins by quoting stock examples from Chinese history of the piety

Of the feelings of savages towards their sick and wounded companions, we rarely hear any

of daughters, and proceeds to ask how it comes to pass, since, in the present day, girls are doubtless equally devoted, that "the female infant is looked upon as an enemy from the moment of its birth, and no sooner enters the world than it is consigned to the nearest pool of water? Certainly, there are parents who entertain an affection for their female infants, and rear them up; but such number scarcely twenty or thirty per cent. The reasons are, either (1) that the child is thrown away in disgust because the parents have too many children already, or (2) that it is drowned from sheer chagrin at having begotten none but females, or, lastly, in the fear that the poverty of the family will make it difficult to devote the milk to her own child, when the mother might otherwise hire herself out as a wet-nurse. Now, all these are the most stupid of reasons. All that those have to do who are unable, through poverty, to feed their children, is to send them to the Foundling Hospital, where they will be reared up until they become women and wives, and where they will always be sure of enjoying a natural lifetime. With regard to the question of means or no means of bringing up a family, why, the bare necessaries of life for such children do not cost much. There are cases enough of poor lads not being able to find a wife all their lives long; but the treasurer has yet to hear of a poor girl who cannot find a husband, so that there is even less cause for anxiety on that score. But there is another way of looking at it. Heaven's retribution is sure; and cases are common, where repeated female births have followed those when the infants have been drowned; that is, man loves to slay what heaven loves to beget, and those perish who set themselves against heaven, as those die who take human life. Also they are haunted by the wraiths of the murdered children, and thus not only fail to hasten the birth of a male child, but run a risk of making victims of themselves by their behavior. The late governor, hearing that this wicked custom was rife in Hupei, set forth the law, some time ago, in

anecdotes.[1] I have failed to meet one illustrative of pity or tenderness. Their emotions on witnessing the pleasures, feastings, and marriages of others, seem usually to partake of the character of restless and envious disquietude, visible in dogs when their companions are petted, or possessed of a supernumerary bone.

Passing now from the brute and the savage, we must inquire whether any faint trace of

severe prohibitory proclamations: notwithstanding this, many poor districts and out-of-the-way places will not allow themselves to see what is right, but obstinately cling to their old delusion. Hia Chien-yin, a graduate from Kianghia, and others, have lately petitioned that a proclamation be issued once more, prohibiting this practice in strong terms. Wherefore you are now required and requested to acquaint yourselves all, that, male and female infants being of your own flesh and blood, you may be visited by some monstrous calamity, if you rear only the male, and drown the female children. If these exhortations are looked upon any more as mere formal words; and if any people with conscious wickednesss neglect to turn over a new leaf, they will be punished.

"Beware and obey! Beware!"

[1] Dr. Johnson *loq.*: "Pity is not natural to man. Children are always cruel. Savages are always cruel. Pity is acquired and improved by the cultivation of reason. We may have uneasy sensations from seeing a creature in distress, without pity; for we have not pity, unless we wish to relieve them. When I am on my way to dine with a friend, and, finding it late, have bid the coachman make haste, if I happen to attend when he whips his horses, I may feel unpleasantly that the animals are put to pain; but I do not wish him to desist. No, sir, I wish him to drive on." — MAIN'S BOSWELL, p. 120.

heteropathy yet lingers amongst ourselves. Let us take a young child, the offspring of a cultivated English gentleman and tender-hearted English lady, and observe what are the emotions it exhibits when it sees its baby-brother receive an injury, and cry aloud in pain. That child's sentiments are, we cannot doubt, considerably modified from those of its barbarian ancestors,

> "When wild in woods the noble savage ran,"

just as the instincts of the kitten of a domestic cat, or puppy of a lap-dog, differ from those of the cub of a cat-o'-mountain, or the whelp of a wolf. Even yet, however, an impartial study may leave us room to hesitate before we "count the gray barbarian" so very far "lower than the Christian child," as that no signs of savage impulse shall now and then betray the old leaven in the curled darling of the British nursery. If narrowly watched, at least one child out of two or three will be seen to be very abnormally excited by the sight of his brother's pain. He will appear much as if subjected to an electric shock; and his behavior will be found to partake, in an unaccountable way, of all the characteristics of anger and annoyance against the sufferer. There is no softness or tenderness in the looks which he casts at his companion; nor will he, usually, spontaneously make the slightest effort to help or comfort him by the caresses which he is wont to lavish on him to excess at other moments. On the contrary, a disposition will generally be manifested to add, by a good hard blow, or sharp vicious scratch, to the woe of his unfortunate friend. There may be — indeed, there will usually occur — a burst of tears like a thunder-shower; but the character of this weeping-fit is that of an explosion of irritation and disgust, rather than of pity or fellow-feeling. A gentle and affectionate little girl of three years old has been seen by the writer to exhibit these emotions of heteropathy as distinctly as any angry bull or cannibal savage. The child's baby-sister of two years old fell off the lofty bed on which both were amicably playing, and, of course, set up a wail of fright and pain on the floor. Instantly the elder child let herself slip down on the opposite side, ran round the bed, and pounced on the poor little one on the floor, whom she proceeded incontinently to belabor violently with both hands, before rescue could arrive. Of course, eventually both parties joined in a roar: but the baby's was a wail of pain and terror; the elder child's, a tempest of indignation. Mothers and nurses, on being strictly interrogated, will generally confess to having witnessed similar unmistakable symptoms of heteropathy still lurking in the sweetest-tempered children. The sight of the pain-distorted features of their friends, or the moans of an invalid, often call forth very ugly emotions; and, though many tender-natured babies show trouble at the tears of their elders, even they are generally more excited than depressed when they chance to witness any solemn scene or demonstrative grief. Fond mothers naturally explain all such disagreeable exhibitions as resulting from the inability of innocent little children to understand pain and sorrow. But the fact is, that they do, to a certain extent, understand what they see; but the exalted emotion of reflected sympathy is yet lacking, and, in place of it, there are traces of the merely animal and savage instinct. Of course, the infantine displays of anger and irritation are instantly checked in civilized homes; and the imitative faculty is enlisted, during its earliest and most vigorous period, on the side of compassion, which is often enough foolishly misapplied and exaggerated, till, by the time the little girl is four or five years old, she is so far trained as to endure paroxysms of woe for the misadventures of her doll deprived of an eye, or exposed to the martyrdom of St. Lawrence before the nursery fire. The "hereditary transmission of psychical habits" has also obviously, in many cases, resulted in the inheritance of genuine sympathy, even from the cradle. The old heteropathy has been, strictly speaking, "bred out."

In a similar though less marked manner, the sight of another person's pleasure produces, in the childish and yet uncultured mind, something much more like displeasure than reflex happiness. Apart from the sense of injustice in the distribution of toys, food, or caresses (of course a fertile source of infantile jealousy), there is an actual irritation at the spectacle of another's enjoyment, and a disposition to detract from it, — to destroy the toy, or spoil the food, or disturb the caresses, — forming the most perfect antithesis to the reflected delight in, and desire to enhance, another's pleasure, which constitute the sympathy of adult life. Of course, here, also, education generally steps in to check the display, if not to eradicate the sentiment, of envy, which, as La Rochefoucauld says, is the only one of all human passions in which no one takes pride, and which, therefore, its most abject victims soon learn carefully to cloak. But enough of it is betrayed in every schoolroom and playground to corroborate the assertion that our earliest emotion is not pleasure in another's pleasure, any more than pain in another's pain.

May we stop here? Does true sympathy invariably fill the breasts of all grown-up men and women in a civilized land, so as to leave no room for heteropathy, either in its form of irritation at pain, or disgust at pleasure? Alas! it is to be feared that a stern self-scrutiny would permit few of us to boast that there are no impulses resembling these left in our nature to testify to their ancient sway. There are not many men whom the tears of a woman, or the wail of an infant, do not irritate, and who have no need of self-control to avoid giving expression to anger at such sights or sounds. To many more, and even to some women, the spectacle of disease and feebleness is naturally so repugnant, that the effort to render help must always be stimulated by some potent affection, interest, or sense of duty, — a fact, we may parenthetically observe, which merits the serious attention of that "Noodledom" which Sydney Smith says is "never tired of repeating, that the proper sphere of woman is the sick-room," and assumes that every human female is a heaven-made nurse.

Among the lower classes of society, the emotion of heteropathy unmistakably often finds its terrible vent in the violence of husbands to wives, and of parents, step-parents, and schoolmasters, to children. Carefully scanning the police reports, it will be seen that the rage of the criminal (usually half drunk, and guided by instinct alone) is excited by the precise objects which would wring his heart with pity, had he attained the stage of genuine sympathy. The group of shivering and starving children and weeping wife is the sad sight, which, greeting the eyes of the husband and father reeling home from the gin-shop, somehow kindles fury in his breast. If the baby cry in its cradle, he stamps on it: if his wife wring her hands in despair, and implore him to give her bread for their children, he fells her with his fist, or perhaps (as in a recent notorious case) holds her on the fire till she is burned past recovery. Again: as regards the no less horrible crime of cruelty practised by both men and women (especially as step-parents) upon children, it may be always observed, that from the moment in which an unfortunate little creature has fallen behind its brothers and sisters in physical or mental strength, or received an unjustly severe punishment, from thenceforth its weakness and sobs, its crouching and timid demeanor, and at last its attenuated frame and joyless young face (the very sights which almost break a compassionate heart to behold), prove only provocations to its natural guardians to fresh outrage and chastisement. The feebler and more miserable the child grows, the more malignant is the heteropathy of its persecutors, till the neighbors (often so criminally inert!) wonder "what has come to them" to behave so barbarously. The truth is, that here, in the yet lingering shades of the old savage passion, we find the explanation of a familiar but most hideous mystery in our nature,—the fact that cruelty grows by what it feeds on; that, the more a tyrant causes his victim to suffer, the more he hates him, and revels in the sight of his anguish. Beside the deep-seated sting of self-reproach, which has been generally supposed to goad the cruel man to hate those whom he has injured (just as self-complacency makes the philanthropist love the object of his beneficence), the cruel person is always lashed by his own heteropathy to hate his victim exactly *in proportion* to his sufferings. The boor who has, perhaps almost unconsciously, struck some wretched woman who bears his burdens, grows savage if he see her bleed or faint, and repeats the blow with redoubled violence, till the moment comes in which he suddenly recognizes that the object of his rage can suffer no more, when his passion instantly collapses, and he seems to waken out of a dream. Just in a parallel way, in the higher walks of life, moral cruelty develops itself in proportion as the victim betrays the anguish caused by cutting words and unkind acts, and receives its check only when a real or feigned indifference shields the suffering heart from further wounds.

If we go yet a step further, and note the emotions raised in the breast of men of the ruder sort at the sight of the pain and death of animals, there can be little doubt that the existence of thoroughly savage heteropathy may often be traced among the cruelties of slaughter-houses, whale and seal fisheries, bull-fights and dog-fights, and even among many field-sports of a better kind.

The rudimentary form of reflex emotion, where it concerns pleasure, is somewhat more difficult to trace than where it meets with pain. The envy [1] candidly exhibited by children, animals,

[1] The Chinese, to justify the sentiment, have framed the ingenious theory, that there exists only a fixed quantity of happiness for mankind to partake, and that, consequently, when A is happy, B is authorized to consider himself defrauded. The late amiable and gifted statesman, Cavaliere Massimo d'Azeglio, who had singularly favorable opportunities for comparing English and Italian public life, remarked to the writer, that *invidia* unhappily pervaded Italian poli-

and savages, as before remarked, is carefully veiled in civilized and adult life; but undoubtedly it prevails everywhere to an extent sadly inimical to the existence of genuine reflected pleasure. For reasons to be hereafter stated, however, it would appear that the development of true sympathy with pleasure precedes chronologically that of similar sympathy with pain.

Starting now from the position, which I hope may have been sufficiently established, that the earliest reflected emotion is not sympathetic pain with pain, nor yet pleasure with pleasure, but heteropathic resentment towards pain, and displeasure towards pleasure, our next task is to attempt to define the stages by which these crude and cruel emotions pass into the tender and beneficent sentiment. That this transition is not only exceedingly slow, but also altogether irregular, is obvious at first sight. There are

ties to a degree almost inconceivable to an Englishman. Even a success, he said, such as a battle gained, or a powerful speech made in the Chamber, was a source of danger to a minister, owing to the enmity it excited, even among his own partisans. In France, the immense success of the insurance-offices is attributed to the value of their *plaques*, placed prominently on a house as a protection against malicious arson. And in Normandy, of very recent years, the inhabitants of several districts have adopted the use of tiles, instead of thatch, avowedly to save themselves from the dangers arising from the envy of neighbors and relatives.

two things to be accomplished simultaneously,—the sentiment itself must alter its character from cruel to kind; and secondly, having become kind, it must extend its influence, according to Pope's beautiful simile, in ever-widening circles,

> "As a small pebble stirs some peaceful lake."

Practically, we find that the sentiment is always unequally developed in character, and also extended in an erratic and unaccountable manner, not at all in symmetric circles, but in irregular polygons, with which no geometry of the affections can deal. Nay, there would appear to be almost insuperable difficulties in the way of a simultaneous development in warmth and in expanse of sympathy. He who feels passionately for his friends rarely embraces the wider range of social and national interests; and he who extends his philanthropy to whole classes and continents too often proves incapable of that strong individual love of which the poet could boast,

> "Which, like an indivisible glory, lay
> On both our souls, and dwelt in us
> As we did dwell in it,"—

the most beautiful sentiment in human nature,

and the most blessed joy, next to the joy of divine love, in human life.[1]

How the destructive and cruel instincts began of old to modify themselves is naturally a very obscure problem, on which even Mr. Bagehot's ingenious and valuable speculations regarding the early crystallization of society can throw little light. The process of amelioration must have advanced considerably, even before a polity, in any sense, can have existed. From the first, the human mother, like the mother bird and brute, no doubt felt "compassion for the son of her womb," even though her pity lamentably failed to prevent her concurrence in infanticide in the cases most calling for that compassion. From the tenderness of mothers must have radiated, as from a focus, the protective instincts in each family; the father sharing them in a secondary degree. In the earliest savage state, except for such parental love, those affections defined by the schoolmen as the complacent, as distinguished from the benevolent, must have had it all their own way. The man loved the persons who ministered to

[1] That it is not impossible, though singularly rare, for a man to unite the character of an ardent philanthropist with that of a most affectionate husband, father and friend, will be readily conceded by the many who mourn the recent death of Matthew Davenport Hill.

his pleasure, not those who called on him for self-sacrifice. Still, even through such wholly selfish love, we must suppose him to have begun to realize in his dim imagination the pain he witnessed in a beloved person, and, having once figured it as his own, to have regarded the sufferer with softened feelings. Possibly, in some cases, this newly-born emotion may at once have taken the shape of helpful sympathy. The "brave" who saw his companion wounded may have carried him off the field, plucked out the spear-head from his side, or quenched his burning thirst with water. More often, and as a general rule, however, it may be suspected that a long interval has taken place after the destructive instinct is checked before the protective one arises; and in this interval the emotion exhibited is that which I shall class as the second in the development of the feelings; namely, *aversion.*

Pursuing our method of seeking illustrations from the animal world, we find that several of the gentler brutes, and such as have seemed to receive some influence from the companionship of civilized man, very often display this aversion to their sick and suffering companions. They forsake and shun them, instead of goring, or tearing them to pieces. Among such species, the diseased creature itself is so well aware of the instincts of its kind, that, without waiting to be "sent to Coventry," it shrinks into some out-of-the-way corner to hide its misery from their unfeeling eyes, though, in the very same distress, it will seek out a human friend, and deliberately call his attention to its sad state, obviously with full confidence that he will gladly afford relief.

Just in the same way, young children very often testify aversion to grown people of mournful aspect, or who bear the traces of suffering on their features. As a general rule, they shrink from the sight of pain, and run from it to hide their faces in their mothers' lap. A little girl brought to visit a lady whom she had been accustomed to see strong and active, but who had become a cripple, burst into a passion of tears at the sight of her crutches, and could not be persuaded to approach or look at her again. Perhaps few of us, even in after-life, could boast that we have wholly outgrown this phase of feeling, and that we invariably experience the impulse of the Samaritan, and not that of the Levite or the priest, when any specially deplorable spectacle lies by the side of our way. Certainly the pleasure-loving nations of the south of Europe have by no means arrived at such a stage of progress, but habitually abandon even the house wherein father or mother, wife, brother, or child, is lying in life's last piteous struggle, aided only by the muttered prayers of the priest at the bed-foot, and without a loving hand to wipe the death-sweat from the brow, or a human breast on which to rest the fainting head. That the childish fears of Italians concerning infection from such diseases as consumption has something to do with this shameful cowardice (prevalent under all circumstances, and in every class, from the highest to the lowest, throughout the peninsula) may be probable. And that the monopoly of religious consolation by the Romish priesthood, and their jealousy of all lay interference with the position into which they thrust themselves between each soul and its Maker, has encouraged and sanctioned it, till it has become an indisputable custom, there can be little doubt. Nevertheless, we have assuredly here, among one of the most gifted and warm-hearted of nations, an illustration, on the largest scale, of the fact I am endeavoring to bring forward; namely, that aversion to the suffering and dying is an emotion having a place in the historical development of human feeling, no less marked than the heteropathy which preceded it.

If my theory of development be correct, this sentiment of aversion must, at a certain stage of progress, have been the prevailing one; and perhaps I shall do no injustice to Mr. Gladstone's dearly-loved Homeric Greeks, if I surmise that they had approximately reached that era, and stood, in the matter of sentiment, about halfway between the prehistoric savage and the English gentleman. Among the former, Philoctetes would have been speared or stoned to death. Had he lived in our time, and served on those same shores in British ranks, he would have been tenderly conveyed to a hospital; and a band of high-born ladies from his native land would have traversed the seas to nurse him. The actual comrades of Philoctetes took, or (what comes to the same thing) are represented by their poets as taking, neither one course nor the other. They felt aversion to their miserable companion in his horrible suffering, and accordingly banished him to Lemnos, where even Sophocles is content to represent him howling over his anguish and desertion as quite in the natural order of things.

Throughout the whole millennium before the birth of Christ, we may dimly discern among the nations of East and West the struggle which was going forward. If aversion were probably the predominant sentiment towards distress, sympathy was beginning to work freely, and heteropathy still remained as a stupendous power. The most ancient literature — the Rig-Veda, the Zendavesta, and the Hebrew Scriptures — reaches back to no period before sympathy was in full exercise, and had received the solemn sanction of religion. Among the Hebrews (or perhaps, in the special case, we must say the Chaldæans), the sense of sympathy with pain and misfortune reigned, at all events, as early as the days of Job, whose friends, unlike those of Philoctetes, flocked ostensibly to mourn with him, albeit their sympathy was injudiciously expressed, and bears some tokens of that disposition to add moral to physical suffering, which is a refined form of heteropathy. It took several centuries more before Euripides, the most sentimental of the Greeks, could go so far as to say, —

"'Tis unbecoming not to shed a tear
Over the wretched. He, too, is devoid
Of virtue who abounds in wealth, yet scruples,
Through sordid avarice, to relieve his wants."[1]

And, on the other hand, Hebrews and heathens alike believed that the opposite sentiment of

[1] Antiope.

heteropathy towards the sufferings of *enemies* was divinely sanctioned, and that, in a word, the principle to be acted upon was, "Thou shalt love thy neighbor, and hate thine enemy." Few modern readers can have failed to remark the extraordinary share which those "enemies," against whom it was lawful to pray, seem to take in the concerns of the Psalmists, and perhaps to have wondered whether the thoughts of any men of similar piety and exalted feeling in these days are ever occupied in the like way.

Among the Gentile nations, no subjects of art seem to have pleased the Assyrians and Egyptians better than the impalings and flayings of captives,—cruelties which, had they been committed by a modern army, would certainly not have been reproduced in painting or sculpture. A great revolution in feeling must have occurred between the ages when Sennacherib and Rameses desired to be immortalized in connection with such atrocities, and that when Marcus Aurelius chose that his magnificent equestrian statue on the Capitoline Hill should represent him in the act of protecting his captives from the violence of his Legions.

Not only art, but the very language of the ancient world, preserves the traces of the cruel heteropathy of old, as the rocks the fossil teeth of the saurians,

> "Which tare each other in their slime."

It shocks us to imagine the disciple of Socrates, "whose benevolence," as Xenophon wonderingly remarks, "even extended to all mankind," wandering amid the groves of the Academy discussing all the loftiest themes of human thought, and at the same time talking incidentally of *ἐπιχαιρεκακία* as of an every-day and familiar passion. Yet this was the case even in "sacred Athens," where

> "Near the fane
> Of Wisdom, Pity's altar stood,"—

an altar which Demonax said would need to be overthrown, were the cruel Roman games to be introduced into the city. Between "rejoicing in the misfortunes of others," and enjoying a gladiatorial show, there was not much to choose in the way of sympathetic emotion.

Passing from Greece to Rome, we find the whole population, at the close of the republic, and the era of the Cæsars, mad with enthusiasm for the exhibitions, held in every town in the empire, of men killing one another by scores, or thrown to be devoured by beasts. Marvellous is the story that the very same populace which clamored for these *circenses* as for bread, filled the theatre with shouts of applause, when Terence first gave expression to that sense of the claims of all human beings to sympathy, which has since played so large a part in the history of our race: —

"Homo sum, humani nihil a me alienum puto."

Something within those stony Roman breasts echoed, like Memnon's statue, to the kindling rays of the rising sun; but we should deceive ourselves widely, if we imagined that any thing resembling our sense of the claims of human brotherhood was then, or for ages afterwards, commonly understood. The precept of Sextius the Pythagorean (preserved by Stobæus) — "Count yourself the care-taker of all men under God" — is almost an anachronism still, if we place the author in the Augustan age, and critically incredible at the earlier date when it was formerly supposed to have been written. The current feeling of the contemporaries of Cato and Cicero, Tacitus and Pliny, received no shock from the most hideous cruelties hourly practised on slaves and captives of war. Nor did there then exist in Europe a single hospital for the sick, or asylum for the destitute, the blind, or the insane; the first institution of the kind known in history being a hospital, built in the fifth century, in Jerusalem, for monks driven mad by asceticism; and one of the next earliest, a foundling hospital opened in Milan in 789. Organized cruelty was in full force; but organized charity was yet unknown. And the wealthy Herodes Atticus, the proto-philanthropist, found no better way to display his beneficence than by building the splendid theatre whose ruins still crumble in the shadow of the Athenian Acropolis.

And here we fall on the natural explanation of a fact mentioned a few pages ago. The emotion of pleasure in another's pleasure, though usually fainter than the parallel sympathy with pain, seems to have been historically the soonest developed, — at all events, among the sunny-spirited nations of the South, with whom classic history is concerned. The Greeks and Romans "rejoiced with those who did rejoice" much sooner and more readily than they "wept with those who wept." "Væ victis!" the vulture-shriek of heteropathy, echoes through the night of time, across the arenas where slaughtered gladiators, and Christians mangled by the lions, made the "glory of a Roman holiday." But even that hideous triumph may be interpreted as, in some sort, the expression of sympathy felt for the successful swordsman, or for the ravenous wild beast. The pain (if any could be said to exist) of beholding so pitiful a sight as that which the statue of the Dying Gladiator recalls, or the still worse horror of watching a tiger's carnival, was lost to the fierce Roman heart in the joy of triumph with the victor. Is all this utterly inconceivable to us? The bull-fights of Spain exhibit to the present day precisely analogous phenomena. The spectacle of a miserable horse gored to death, and dragged along, leaving his entrails strewed across the arena, has been witnessed scores of times with supreme indifference by men and women, noble and imperial, engrossed by sympathetic delight in the skill of the *toreador*, or even in the courage of the poor maddened bull, whose dying agony afforded the next instant's pleasure.

Even in our own field-sports, whence cruelty has been eliminated to the uttermost, the most tender-hearted of fox-hunters and fowlers tell us that they sympathize so much with the hounds, that they have no time to feel for the fox; and share so keenly the pleasure of their pointers in a day on the moors, that the brief death-pangs of the grouse are unnoticed. In the earlier ages, it would seem as if pleasure in the pleasure of others, particularly in the pleasure of victory, always outran pain in the pain of the vanquished. It asked the deeper sentiment of the "dark and true and tender North," the tenderness breathed all through Christianity from the spirit of its Founder, perchance even the accumulated experience of suffering, ploughing deep through generations into the race, as a single experience ploughs up, and makes soft the individual heart, — it needed all these to enable men to feel other men's pain as their own.

Be it also borne in mind, that sympathy with pleasure, usually demanding of us far less sacrifice than sympathy with pain (indeed generally demanding no sacrifice at all), obtains its way, necessarily, sooner than the sentiment which must rise high enough to compel self-sacrifice before it becomes manifest. The proverbial readiness of Englishmen to espouse the weaker cause implies more stringent, as well as nobler emotion, than the spaniel-like readiness of slavish races to attack the beaten, and side with the strong. Of course, such heroism, like every other good deed, brings its reward in a fresh sense of sympathy towards those who have been protected. The roots of the tree of human love are nourished by the fallen leaves of kind actions which sprung from its heart, and have long dropped and been forgotten.

While the slow progress above described was going on, a singular limitation may be observed among those to whom sympathy was extended. Among the indubitable results of recent ethnological research is the discovery, that in early times, and to this day among savages, such affectionate sentiments and notions of moral obligation as are yet developed are entirely confined to the *tribe*. Beyond the tribe, robbery, plunder, rape, and assassination, are never understood to be offences, and are frequently considered as meritorious, much as tiger-shooting is deemed laudable and public-spirited among ourselves. There is a line of circumvallation, outside of which kindly feeling does not extend, and the moral obligations which concern such feeling are consequently not imagined to apply. Within the line, there is brotherhood, and certain recognized rules of action, rising, by degrees, from the mere prohibition of perfidy, murder, and adultery, to the inculcation of truth and helpfulness, extending to the very borders of communism. Outside the line, all the while, the "Gentile," the "Barbarian," the man of alien blood, is not merely less considered (as is the case between ourselves and foreigners), but has actually no *status* at all, either as regards feeling or duty. The step over this barrier of race, when it begins to be taken, is an enormous stride; and we may see how it was felt as such even by the writers of the New Testament. This subject, however, is far too large to be here treated otherwise than by briefest indication. No doubt the union of the known world in one empire in the Augustan age helped to give birth to the great idea of a common humanity, with universal claims to sympathy, which, as I have remarked, at that time first arose. The simile of the body and its members occurred alike to St. Paul and to Cicero,[1] to express the mutual suffering of men in the woes of their kind; and from thenceforth the enthusiasm of humanity may be said to have been kindled, though as yet but a spark.

But, from the hour that the idea of a common humanity with universal claims dawned on the minds of men, the question, "Who is human?" appears to have arisen; just as the Pharisee, when commanded to "love his neighbor," asked, "Who is my neighbor?" From that

[1] De Off. iii. 5.

distant date, till the day (not yet a decade ago) when the Supreme Court of the United States decreed that "a negro was not a man under the terms of the Constitution," there has been a ceaseless effort to shut out inferior and inimical races from the title which was felt to carry with it the claims of brotherhood. In the pre-historic and earliest historic times, the basis was laid for a great many of the prejudices which survive even yet. When the tall, fair races invaded Europe, and drove the short and dark-haired ones into remote mountains and caves, then began the legends of the giants and the dwarfs; each regarding the other as *non-human*, and fit objects of hatred, and all manner of perfidy and injury. To the tall race, their predecessors were Pygmies and Gnomes, engaged in mysterious arts of metallurgy in the bowels of the hills. To the short race, their lusty conquerors were Monsters, Cyclopes, Giants, ever ready to slay them with clubs, and, perchance, devour them limb by limb. Wonderful is it to reflect that the stories embodying these primeval passions of fear and hatred have actually borne down to us in their course, through the traditions of thousands of years, so much of their original sentiment, that every child amongst us to this hour entertains the belief that it is quite right and proper to play perfidious tricks on a dwarf; and that the sanguinary achievements of Jack the Giant-killer, Jack of the Bean-Stalk, and Tom Thumb, against the most unoffending giants, were altogether laudable and glorious! Which of our readers (we beg to ask the question with due seriousness) can, even in adult years, lay his hand on his heart, and say he should feel any moral or sentimental objection to murdering a "Giant" in cold blood, or running a red-hot stake into his solitary eye? As to Ogres, the case is worse. If those archæologists be right, who say that the word is the same as Hogres, Hongres, Hungarians, Huns, we have here, in the full daylight of history, a peculiarly noble European race, actually transformed by the imagination of their neighbors into such preternaturally horrible monsters, that even our uncharitable feelings towards Giants fade into mildness beside our animosity towards an Ogre.

As our own ancestors felt towards the earlier races of Europe, as the old Vedic Aryans felt to the Dasyus (their dark-skinned enemies), as the Mazdiesnans of Zoroaster felt to the Touranians, so, it would seem, existing savage tribes still feel to races far apart from their own in blood, but having neighboring habitations.

Among numerous anecdotes illustrative of such sentiments, none are more horrible than those which tell of the hatred of the red men for the Esquimaux. A case is recorded where a tribe of the former travelled two or three hundred miles over the snow for the sole purpose of destroying a village of the inoffensive Esquimaux, with whom they had no quarrel, and who possessed no property worth their robbery. As a dog kills a rat, so do such races destroy each other, under an impulse of pure hatred, which, perhaps, had its origin in the heteropathy of conquering generations ages before. Probably, in its earlier stages, every nation now existing has thus had its detested "Canaanite" dwelling on the borders of the land, and credited with every inhuman vice and crime.[1]

Parallel, and nearly contemporaneously, with the idea of a common humanity, arose the idea of a common Christianity, forming the bond of still more sacred mutual sympathy. It would be to rewrite the history of the last eighteen centuries to record how this new im-

[1] "The almost physical loathing which a primitive community feels for men of widely different manners from its own, usually expresses itself by describing them as monsters, such as giants, or even (as is almost always the case in Oriental mythology) as demons. The Cyclopes is Homer's type of an alien." —MAINE'S *Ancient Law*, p. 125.

pulse has drawn together the hearts of men in twofold fashion. Inwardly, the deeper spiritual life which then was awakened, and with it the peculiarly softening influence of penitence, must have effected much; while the apotheosis of suffering, in the ever-recurrent emblem of the cross, cannot have failed (as Mr. Lecky eloquently describes it) to have trained to sentiments of compassion the rough races who substituted it for the images of Thor and Woden, or of Mars and Zeus. Outwardly, a welding no less obvious has been effected by the organization of a "Christendom," begun among all the tender associations of the little band in the "upper chamber," and continued through ages, "when the disciples had all things in common," and in those wherein they endured together the Ten Persecutions, and finally completed in the era when antagonism with Islam united all the Christian nations in the Crusades. A similar, though perhaps less forcible, influence of the outward kind was meanwhile effected outside the Christian camp, among the nations which accepted the creed of Mahomet, whose levelling tendency (like that of Buddhism) has probably scarcely less aided the growth of mutual sympathies among its disciples than the presentation of a common object of worship, and the direct inculcation of mercy and beneficence. As the present condition of India unhappily exemplifies, caste is, of all barriers, the most insurmountable to the sympathies of mankind. All the great religions of the East, however, and pre-eminently Zoroastrianism and Buddhism, have contributed importantly to the nourishment of the sympathetic affections, by stamping them with approval, and condemning any manifestation of the opposite sentiments. When men in each nation have risen so high as to recognize the benevolence of God, they have always embodied that truth in creeds, wherein God is represented as commanding men to be benevolent; and these crystallized creeds have acted with compact and persistent force on the future development of the benevolent affections. In each case, we must needs account, in the first place, *outside* of conscious or recognized religious influences, and in the region of the secret divine education of the race, for the development of those social sentiments, which, as all ethnology proves, are not in the earliest stage understood to have any connection with the worship of the unseen powers.

Returning to the history of such feelings in Christendom, we find, that, just as the title of "human" was refused to inimical races as soon as a common humanity was understood to convey the right to sympathy, so the claim of Christian brotherhood was still more jealously refused to all outside the pale of the Catholic Church. Pity for Jews, Turks, Infidels, or Heretics, there was little or none during all the ages wherein that great Church maintained its unity unbroken. To torture the Jew, to slay the Saracen, and to burn the Heretic, were actions not only laudable (as the primitive savage thought it laudable to slay the enemies of his tribe), but religiously obligatory. The Church had taken the place of the tribe; and the feelings it inspired and sanctioned were even more vivid, alike for good and for evil.

At last the Reformation came, and with it fresh questionings as to whom the fold of Christian brotherhood should include. The Protestants — themselves outside the pale of Roman fraternity — found Quakers, Socinians, and Anabaptists, to exclude from their own, and, still farther off, a hundred thousand hapless witches and wizards to thrust beyond the limits even of humanity. At last the fires of hate and fear died down; and, for a century and a half, true sympathy has been permitted to grow up amongst us comparatively unchecked. The result is, that the sense of Christian brotherhood has perhaps more force amongst us than ever before, while the enthusiasm of humanity (extending far, and experienced intensely, altogether beyond the bounds of the churches) has risen to the height when a passion becomes self-conscious, and receives baptism, evermore to take its place among the recognized sentiments of our race. If a barrier to perfect sympathy among men be now anywhere left standing, we acknowledge unanimously that it is a blot on our civilization, and, so far from being in accordance with our religion, is in defiance thereof.

From destructive heteropathy to negative aversion, and thence to positive and helpful sympathy, — such has been the progress in the *character* of the emotion I have now endeavored to trace from the dawn of history till the present time. From the tribe to the nation, to the homan race, to the whole sentient creation, — such has been the progress in *extension* of that sympathy as it gradually developed itself. Neither line of progress is yet nearly completed. Much heteropathy still lingers amongst us. Aversion to the suffering and miserable is even yet a common sentiment; and our sympathy, such as it is, might be far warmer, and better sustained. Nor is the lateral expansion of our fellow-feeling any way uniform, or co-extensive with our knowledge. There must, of course, from the limitations of our natures, be always a more vivid emotion raised by a neighboring than by a remote catastrophe. None but He who is alike near to all can sympathize with all alike. But making every allowance for the inevitable partialities of nationality and neighborhood, and the comparatively easy comprehension of the joys and sorrows of persons of our own age, race, and class, it would seem that there is yet great room for further and more equable development. Along every plane on which our feelings run, they as yet come short. In the first place, even as regards local and national extension, the just proportion between the near and the remote, the concerns of our countrymen and those of others, is very far from being represented by the various degrees of interest manifested by the British public when it reads of the burning of a warehouse in London, cr the conflagration of a city in America; of a boat upset on the Isis, or of the suffocation of the whole crew of a Chinese junk; of a breeze off the Goodwins, or of a hurricane in Bengal; of a scarcity of water in a Kentish village, or of the depopulation of whole provinces by famine in Persia.

Secondly, it is not only geographically and

laterally that our sympathies fail in extension, but also, and much more emphatically, *perpendicularly* (if we may so express it), through the various strata of society. Our class-sympathies (especially at both ends of the scale) are as strong as our national sympathies, and, more than they, need to be widened. The high-bòrn Englishman feels more akin to the German, Italian, or Russian noble than to the small tradesman or peasant of his own country; and the rise of the perilous International affords singular proof how far the working-classes are beginning to feel their cosmopolitan class-sympathies override their patriotism. A great deal, however, has been done during this century, on the other hand, towards the breaking-down of the barriers which limited the more tender emotions to different ranks. Free and cordial association is far more common everywhere; and the failure to sympathize outside of a man's own class is now (as it ought to be) more often noticeable among the uneducated or half-educated than the cultured.

The literature of two generations past recalls the yet recent period when any thing like "sentiment" was supposed to be the exclusive attribute of well-born and well-mannered people, and when no novelist would have dreamed of asking for sympathy in the woes of any "common person." There were gentlemen, indeed, of whom "Tremaine" was the archetype, and ladies who lived on air and Æolian harps; and there were also beggars and shepherdesses; but of the intermediate classes of cotton-spinners, clerks, bakers, ironmongers, bricklayers, needlewomen, and housemaids, it had never entered into anybody's head, in the pre-Dickens age, that any thing affecting could be written. Even Shakspeare himself had looked, like a born aristocrat, not unkindly, but somewhat jestingly, at such subjects; and though we cannot doubt, that, in real life, there must have been far more of mutual sympathy than books betray, it is tolerably certain there was infinitely less readiness to feel for vulgar sorrows, and rejoice in homely joys, than, thank God! is now to be found amongst us. The writers who have helped us to this tenderer feeling for human nature under its less refined forms — writers such as Dickens and Mrs. Gaskell and Mrs. Stowe — deserve even more honor than those who, like Miss Bremer and d'Azeglio and George Sand and Richter, have aided us to sympathize with the inner life of other nations.

There yet remain to be noticed other directions in which our sympathies extend themselves very irregularly. As a general rule, the tenderest of all feelings are those between persons of opposite sexes; and the differences which exist, so far from diminishing sympathy, probably often enhance it. Nevertheless, the position of women in the East, and even in Europe, offers irrefragable evidence, that, with all their lavish affection, men have not, on the whole, been able to sympathize with women as with one another. They have been ready enough to indulge their pleasure-loving propensities, their vanity, and their indolence; but those nobler aspirations after instruction and usefulness, which many of them must always have shown, — aspirations which men remark with the most ardent and helpful sympathy when displayed by boys, — have rarely touched them in women. No man will give his son a stone when he asks for bread; but thousands of men have given their daughters diamonds when they prayed for books, and coiled the serpents of dissipation and vanity round their necks, when they needed the wholesome food of beneficent employment.

On the other hand, though women cannot be accused of any general want of sympathy with men, yet they, too, bestow it often in a weak and unworthy manner, rejoicing in their lower pleasures, and suffering with their lower pains, but having little fellow-feeling with their loftier aims, or regrets for their sadder failures. "Rosamond Vincy" would have doubtless shed abundant tears over "Lydgate's" misfortune, had he broken his arm. She had not a sigh to give to his shattered aspirations.

And yet, again, besides the imperfect sympathy of men and women for each other, there is, very commonly, failure in the sympathy of both for children. With all the fondness of parents and relatives, numberless poor little creatures pass through the springtime of life exposed to very nipping winds, so far as their feelings are concerned, though perhaps all the time mentally and physically precociously forced in a hot-bed of high culture. Because their pains are mere childish pains, we find it hard to pity them; and their little pleasures, because they are so simple, seem only to deserve from us a patronizing smile, or the warning "not to be foolish and excited," which often quenches the joyous little spirit most effectually. But, as St. Augustine truly says, the boy's sufferings, while they last, are quite as real as those of the man: indeed, few of us have troubles much worse, even now, than punishment and heavy tasks. And as to the pleasures of those young years when all earth seemed paradise, and every sense was an inlet of fresh delight, — may we not vainly look round for cause for equal sympathy in the happiness of an adult companion, such as we may find in that of the child playing in the meadow with its cowslip ball, or shouting with ecstasy as its kite soars into the blue summer heaven? Hateful is it to reflect, that, to many a world-worn heart amongst us, the spectacle of such pure joy, instead of awakening that sense of "pleasure in pleasure," which we flatter ourselves is our habitual sentiment, not seldom calls up, on the contrary, an ugly emotion, much more partaking of the character of heteropathy, and provoking us to check the exuberance of the child's delight by some harsh word or peremptory prohibition.

One more observation, and this part of my subject may close. Not only do our sympathies require to be more equally extended as regards nations, classes, sexes, and ages; but there is sore need that they should spread outside the human race, among the tribes of sentient creatures who lie beneath us and at our mercy. The great ideas of a common humanity and a common Christianity, which were at first such noble *extensions* of family and national sympathies, have long acted as *limitations* thereof. To this hour, in all Romish countries, the sneer, "You talk as if the brute were a Christian," or the simple statement, "*Non è Cristiano*," is understood to dispose finally of a remonstrance against overloading a horse, skinning a goat alive, or plucking the quills of a living fowl. The present benevolent pope answered, a few years ago, the request to found a society for prevention of cruelty in Rome, by the formal response (officially delivered through Lord Odo Russell), "that such an association could not be sanctioned by the Holy See, being founded on a theological error; to wit, that Christians owed any duties to animals." Similarly, the limitation of sympathy to humanity caused English moralists of the last century to argue deliberately, that the evil of cruelty to the lower creatures lay solely in the fact that it injured the finer feelings — the *humanity* — of the men who were guilty of it. Even to this hour, it is not rare to hear in cultivated society the fiendish practice of vivisection condemned or excused by reference solely to the hardening of the sentiments of young surgeons, or the benefits which may remotely accrue to some hypothetical human sufferer, the cause of whose disease may, just possibly, be elucidated thereby.[1]

Surveying the position in which we now stand, after reviewing the long progress of the ages, there is much at which to rejoice for the present, much more to hope for the future. The human heart seems more tender than it has been heretofore; and, if so, the gain is one to which all the triumphs of science and art are small in comparison. Our sympathies are yet very imperfect, and very unequally distributed. To one of us, physical pain appeals most forcibly; to another, want; to another, ignorance. Some of us feel for the sorrows of the aged; some for the

1 "The horrors of visisection, often so wantonly and so needlessly practised" (the *anatomia vivorum* which the heathen Celsus reproved as too inhuman to be perpetrated), "the prolonged and atrocious tortures sometimes inflicted in order to procure some gastronomic delicacy, are so far removed from the public gaze, that they exercise little influence on the characters of men. Yet no humane man can reflect on them without a shudder. To bring these things within the range of ethics, to create the notion of duties towards the animal world, has been, so far as Christian countries are concerned, one of the peculiar merits of the last century, and, for the most part, of Protestant nations. Mahometans and Brahmins have in this sphere considerably surpassed the Christians; and Spain and Italy, in which Catholicism has most deeply planted its roots, are even now, probably, beyond all other countries, those in which inhumanity to animals is most wanton and most unrebuked." — EUROPEAN MORALS, vol. ii. p. 187.

helplessness of infancy. One can weep with the mourner; another can joy with the happy. Mental doubts and anguish touch minds which have known their agony; and the aspirations after knowledge and beauty, those which have felt their noble thirst. Some of us feel intensely for human troubles; and others, again, are full of compassion for the harmless brutes, and feel keenly the

> "Sorrow for the horse o'erdriven,
> And love in which the dog has part."

But all these various hues of the same gentle sentiment have their natural explanation in the experience or the idiosyncrasy of those who display them; and if they act only as special *stimulants* to activity, and not as *limitations* of it, they are innocent and even beneficial. Such as they are, also, these inequalities in the distribution of our sympathies tend constantly to reduce themselves to a minimum, seeing that, in every direction, one tender emotion leads imperceptibly to another. We cannot help the child without helping the parent, nor educate the mind without feeding the body, nor in any way cultivate the habit of noting and relieving the wants of others without causing the full tide of our outflowing charity to rise beyond any bounds which we may at first have assigned to it.

In point of strength, we cannot doubt that in our time, in spite of the supposed materialism and selfishness of the age,[1] sympathy has acquired in thousands of generous hearts a very high development indeed. It affords the mainspring of life to a whole army of philanthropists, statesmen, clergymen, sisters of charity, and many more of whom the world never hears. Did the laws of nature permit one person to take the physical pains of another, there would be a constant struggle as to which should bear each wound, each deformity, and each disease. Especially among women, in whom this spirit of loving self-sacrifice is commonly predominant, there would be found at an hour's call a hundred Arrias to tell every shrinking Pætus that "death did not pain," a thousand Alcestes to descend to the grave in the stead of every selfish Admetus. Nay, it may be doubted whether, after a while, the hospitals of the land would contain a single inmate (save, perchance, a few forsaken old women) of those originally

[1] Mr. Bain "approaches the consideration" of that "large region of human feeling," the "tender emotion," by remarking, "This is pre-eminently a glandular emotion. In it, the muscular diffusion is secondary," &c. — THE EMOTIONS, &c., p. 94.

sent there as patients; but every man would go forth, *bailed out*, willingly and joyfully, by mother, sister, wife, or child, remaining to suffer in his stead. Of course, there are special obstacles, as well as special aids, under the new forms of modern life, to the growth and diffusion of sympathy. If literature and steam locomotion, and cheap and rapid postage, and telegraphy, assist immensely to diffuse and to sustain the sympathies of mankind, on the other hand, the vehement struggles for existence and for wealth, and the haste and bustle of our lives, tend almost equally to check and blunt them. If we only compare the amount of feeling which any one of us readily gives to the illness, ruin, or death of a neighbor in the country, and that which we find time to spare to the same misfortunes of another, equally well known and liked, in London, we shall obtain some measure of the influence of the increased rapidity of social circulation on the affections. More difficult is it to estimate the cruel results of the competition for professional advancement, and for "quick returns and large profits," out of which come such offences as the adulterations of food and medicine, the unnatural and portentous extension of the liquor-traffic, and the frightful recklessness of life displayed in the employment of unseaworthy ships. These things are more shocking to the moral sense than the savage atrocities of half-barbarous times, being done, at the instigation of meaner passions, by men far more accountable for their actions. But, though Mr. Ruskin and Mr. Carlyle treat them as the genuine "signs of the times," I am inclined to believe that a better test of our state may be found in the widespread horror and disgust which they have created, and the preponderance, far beyond that of any former age, of public deeds springing unmistakably from the purest enthusiasm of humanity. There are few, I think, who, on calm reflection, will hesitate to admit that there exist less of the antisocial passions, and more of the humane and benevolent ones, now in the world than at any known period of past history.

Beyond all that we have yet attained, we may dimly discern the progress yet to be, and welcome for happier generations the time when a divine and universal sympathy will do its perfect work. Even now there are few of us but must have felt how variable are our powers to feel with others; how, for long periods, our hearts seem shut up in our own interests and pains; and how, again, they seem to open, we know not why, to a sense of the suffering of a friend, a child, a bird, or brute, so keen that it seems a revelation, and every other sorrow and pain we know of acquires new meaning in our eyes, and pierces us as a thorn in our own breasts. There are hours wherein we spontaneously long to do any thing, or suffer any thing, which should mitigate the woes we have suddenly learned to perceive. And, again, there are times when the happiness of others is similarly near and dear to us, and we feel capable of sacrificing all our own joys to secure for them felicity here, and beatitude hereafter. These oscillations of our emotions must surely point to a time in the future growth of humanity wherein that which is now rare shall be frequent, and that which is only occasional shall be habitual. As the whole history of the past shows the gradual dropping-away of the crude and cruel emotions of heteropathy and aversion, and the development of sympathy from its first small seed in the family till it has become the great tree of life which we behold, so, without indulging in Utopian dreams of human perfection, we may reasonably anticipate that the long progress will not stop at that precise step where we find it, but extend yet further indefinitely. As the men of old felt in rare hours of tenderness amid their ceaseless struggles, when "the earth was full of violence and cruel habitations," so the cultured amongst us feel habitually now. And as we feel in our best and tenderest moments, so men in ages to come will likewise feel habitually.

Such gradual rising of the temperature of human sympathy, when it shall take place, will necessarily call into existence a whole new *flora* of kindly deeds and customs to cover the ground of life. Economists are forever looking to improved external organizations to better the conditions of all classes, and these have doubtless their significance and use. But what would be the introduction of the wisest, justest, most perfect political and social organizations which could be planned, compared to the elevation, even by a single degree, of the sense of universal brotherhood, and of the kindly sympathies of man with man? Already we begin to feel that acts of beneficence are scarcely lawful, save when they come as from brother to brother, from the heart of the giver to the hand of the receiver. In the time to come, it is not too much to hope that there will be far less than now of such ungenerous generosity as finds vent in such phrases as, "I have done my duty by him, and now I wash my hands of him;"

"I have done my part, and, if he rot, I care not." Less need even may there be for the deep-sighted Buddhist precept, "If a man cannot feel in charity with another, let him resolve on doing him a kindness, and then he will feel kindly."

And, finally, there seems faintly revealed above the mists wherein we .dwell, the lofty summits of an emotion transcending all that our race yet has experienced, — a sympathy which shall shine on the joys, and melt with the sorrows, not only of the lovely, but of the unlovely, and thus make man at last "perfect as his Father in heaven, who makes his sun to rise on the evil and on the good, and sendeth rain on the just and on the unjust." For eighteen centuries those words have rung in the ears of men; but who can boast he has fathomed their meaning, or conceived any plan of life which could give them practical realization? To do this thoroughly, to feel such genuine sympathy for the stupid, the mean-minded, the vicious, as to enable us to make for them the same sacrifices we should readily make for a beloved friend, — this is to reach that zenith of goodness which the world has idealized in Christ, but towards which scarcely an approximation has been practically made, even by the best of Christians.

What will mortal life be when men come to feel thus? It will be already the fulfilment of the best promise of heaven; for "he that liveth in love liveth in God, and God in him." Mankind will then be joined as in one great insurance against want and woe; and no misfortune will be unbearable to one, because it will be shared by all. So many hearts will rejoice with every innocent joy, that men will live as in a room brightened all round with mirrors reflecting every light. So many hands will stretch forth to alleviate every pain, and remove every burden, and supply every want, that, in the sweet sense of that kindly human love, even the heaviest sorrow will melt away like snow in the sunshine of spring.

Even our poor sympathies, such as they are now, are the source of all our purest joys. Pain and pleasure alike undergo a Rosicrucian transformation from lead to gold, when they pass through the alembic of another's soul; and while the dreariest hell would be entire self-inwrapment, so the sweetest heaven would be to feel as God feels for every creature he has made. When we have advanced a little nearer to such divine sympathy, then it is obvious, also, that we shall be more capable of the supreme joy of divine love, and no longer find the harmony of communion forever broken by the discords of earth. He who will teach us how truly to love the unlovely, will lead us into the land where our sun shall no more go down.

Such is, I believe, the great hope of the human race. It does not lie in the "progress of the intellect," or in the conquest of fresh powers over the realms of nature; not in the improvement of laws, or the more harmonious adjustment of the relations of classes and states; not in the glories of art, or the triumphs of science. All these things may, and doubtless will, adorn the better and happier ages of the future. But that which will truly constitute the blessedness of man will be the gradual dying-out of his tiger passions, his cruelty and his selfishness, and the growth within him of the godlike faculty of love and self-sacrifice; the development of that holiest sympathy wherein all souls shall blend at last, like the tints of the rainbow which the Seer beheld around the great white throne on high.

www.ingramcontent.com/pod-product-compliance
Lightning Source LLC
La Vergne TN
LVHW010232110826
845151LV00004B/1272

* 9 7 8 1 4 2 5 5 2 5 1 7 0 *